Small Talk Englisch

Helga Kansy, PhD

Haufe

Bibliografische Information der Deutschen Bibliothek

Die Deutsche Bibliothek verzeichnet diese Publikation in der Deutschen Nationalbibliografie; detaillierte bibliografische Daten sind im Internet über http://dnb.ddb.de abrufbar.

ISBN 3-448-06168-9
Bestell-Nr. 00811-0001

Postanschrift: Postfach, 82142 Planegg
Hausanschrift: Fraunhoferstraße 5, 82152 Planegg
Fon: (0 89) 8 95 17-0, Fax: (0 89) 8 95 17-2 50
E-Mail: online@haufe.de
Internet www.haufe.de
Lektorat: Gabriele Otto
Redaktion: Sylvia Rein

Umschlaggestaltung: Simone Kienle, par:two büro für visuelles, 70182 Stuttgart
Umschlagentwurf: Agentur Buttgereit & Heidenreich, 45721 Haltern am See
Desktop-Publishing: Agentur: Satz & Zeichen, Karin Lochmann, 83119 Obing
Druck: freiburger graphische betriebe, 79108 Freiburg

Zur Herstellung der Bücher wird nur alterungsbeständiges Papier verwendet.

TaschenGuides – alles, was Sie wissen müssen

Für alle, die wenig Zeit haben und erfahren wollen, worauf es ankommt. Für Einsteiger und für Profis, die ihre Kenntnisse rasch auffrischen wollen:

- Sie sparen Zeit und können das erworbene Wissen effizient umsetzen.
- Kompetente Autoren erklären jedes Thema aktuell, leicht verständlich und praxisnah.
- In der Gliederung finden Sie die wichtigsten Fragen und Probleme aus der Praxis.
- Das übersichtliche Layout ermöglicht es Ihnen, sich rasch zu orientieren.
- Schritt für Schritt-Anleitungen, Checklisten, Beispiele und hilfreiche Tipps bieten Ihnen das nötige Werkzeug für Ihre Arbeit.
- Als Schnelleinstieg in ein Thema ist der TaschenGuide die geeignete Arbeitsbasis für Gruppen in Organisationen und Betrieben.

Ihre Meinung interessiert uns! Mailen Sie einfach an die TaschenGuide-Redaktion unter online@haufe.de. Wir freuen uns auf Ihre Anregungen.

Inhalt

6 **Vorwort**

7 **Das kleine Einmaleins des Small Talk**
8 Meeting and Greeting People / Die Begrüßung
13 Receptions and conferences / Empfänge und Tagungen
16 Invitations / Einladungen
21 Saying Goodbye / Verabschiedung
23 Eating Out / Essen gehen
27 Kulturelle und sprachliche Tipps

35 **Small Talk in the Office / Small Talk im Büro**
36 Conversations in the Office / Bürogespräche
39 Talking about People / Über Personen sprechen
43 Meeting Customers / Kunden willkommen heißen
46 Socializing Events at Work / Gesellige Treffen am Arbeitsplatz
54 Kulturelle und sprachliche Tipps

Cultural and Other Activities / Kulturelle und andere Aktivitäten ■ 59
Theater and Concerts / Theater und Konzerte ■ 60
Film and Literature / Film und Literature ■ 64
Exhibits / Ausstellungen ■ 67
Shopping / Einkaufen ■ 69
Traveling / Unterwegs ■ 73
Kulturelle und sprachliche Tipps ■ 76

Favorite Small Talk Topics / Klassische Small Talk Themen ■ 79
The Weather / Das Wetter ■ 80
Traveling, Cities and Countries / Reisen, Städte und Länder ■ 84
Hobbies and Leisure Activities / Hobbys und Freizeitgestaltung ■ 92
Children, Gardening and Pets / Kinder, Gartenarbeit und Haustiere ■ 97
Sports and Cars / Sport und Autos ■ 106
Kulturelle und sprachliche Tipps ■ 112

List of Useful Expressions / Nützliche Redewendungen ■ 115
Stichwortverzeichnis ■ 125

Vorwort

Während meines Studiums in den USA besuchte ich einen Kurs über Kultur und Kommunikation. Als das Thema Small Talk zur Sprache kam, blinzelte die Professorin mir – der einzigen Deutschen im Kurs – zu und begann die Vorlesung: „Es gibt Kulturen, in denen Small Talk unwichtig ist."

Doch im englischen Sprachraum ist er sehr wichtig! Auf Reisen, bei Geschäftskontakten mit englischsprachigen Partnern, am Telefon oder beim Arbeitsessen sind ein paar Sätze, die ein Gespräch einleiten oder abrunden, Gold wert: Small Talk beeinflusst den gesamten Gesprächsverlauf positiv, erleichtert Absprachen, füllt die Lücken, die entstehen, wenn das eigentliche Gespräch abgeschlossen ist, und baut Brükken zu anderen Themen – und zur menschlichen Seite eines Geschäftspartners. Small Talk ist das wichtigste Mittel, mit anderen unverbindlich ins Gespräch zu kommen und vor allem im Gespräch zu bleiben.

Nur, was sagen Sie auf Stehempfängen, in Kaffeepausen oder beim Abendessen, und vor allem: *Wie* sagen Sie es? Dieser TaschenGuide beantwortet Ihnen diese Fragen durch die Darstellung vielfältiger Gesprächssituationen, durch nützliche Beispielsätze und Redewendungen sowie hilfreiche Tipps zu sprachlichen und kulturellen Besonderheiten. Er hilft Ihnen so, aus Small Talk „big talk" zu machen.

Viel Erfolg dabei wünscht Ihnen

Helga Kansy, PhD

Das kleine Einmaleins des Small Talk

Was bedeutet Small Talk? Wofür ist er notwendig? Small Talk wird mit „Geplauder" übersetzt: Genau das ist immens wichtig, um erste Kontakte mit unbekannten Gesprächspartnern zu knüpfen, um Gespräche einzuleiten und um den richtigen Ton im Umgang mit anderen zu treffen.

Meeting and Greeting People / Die Begrüßung

Der Mensch ist ein Herdentier: Er lebt und überlebt, weil er ständig mit anderen Menschen in Verbindung kommt und mit ihnen kommuniziert. Mimische und gestische Kommunikation spielen dabei zunächst die wichtigste Rolle. Danach folgt die Sprache, aber wichtiger als das, was gesagt wird, ist zunächst, dass etwas gesagt wird, und zwar etwas Nettes, etwas Einladendes, etwas Unverfängliches und durchaus inhaltlich Oberflächliches – Small Talk eben. Auch wenn er im Deutschen oft negativ als „Geschwätz" beurteilt wird, erfüllt der Small Talk die wichtige Funktion der harmlosen Kontaktaufnahme, ohne die jede Party, jedes informelle Treffen, jede ungeplante Begegnung in hilfloses Schweigen mündet.

Der Gruß gehört zu den ritualisierten Redewendungen, die eine Gesprächssituation herstellen. Das deutsche „Grüß Dich" oder „Grüß Sie" wird hierzulande häufig durch ein familiäres Hello! oder das Hi! aus dem amerikanischen Englisch ersetzt. Doch das Englische hat noch weitere Varianten: Good morning oder ganz lässig morning für die Vormittage, good afternoon am Nachmittag und How do you do? (Wie geht es Ihnen?), oft verkürzt zu how d'you do, beim Vorstellen - bis hin zum saloppen Hi everybody, what's new? (Tag allerseits, was gibt's Neues?).

Example 1

Sue: Nice to meet you.
Ron: Nice to meet you, too. I'm Ron.
Sue: My name is Sue. Where are you from?
Ron: I'm from Vienna originally, but I live in Paris now. — ursprünglich
Sue: I see. Those are two beautiful and historic cities, aren't they? — Ich verstehe, aha
Ron: They sure are. I like them both very much. Where are you from? — sicherlich
Sue: Well, I'm from Washington, DC. This is my first time here, what about you?

Example 2

Jeffrey has just started working at the engineering office. He sees a bunch of colleagues chattering by the coffee machine.
Jeffrey: Hello everybody, may I introduce myself? I'm Jeffrey Zach, I just started working on Mr. Crane's project. — darf ich mich vorstellen?
Collegue 1: Hi Jeffrey, Jim Bakula, two doors down, welcome to P&C Engineering. — zwei Türen weiter
Collegue 2: Hello Jeffrey, nice having you here, I'm Sarah, Mr. Olmeyer's secretary. This is Michael Kaminsky, the director of sales. I suppose you've already met? — schön, dass Sie hier sind; Sie kennen sich vermutlich schon?

Useful phrases

Meeting someone for the first time / Jemanden zum ersten Mal treffen

- How are you?
- Nice to meet you. — Freut mich, Sie kennen zu lernen.
- Hi / I'm John.

- My name's ...
- Good morning / afternoon / evening. How do you do?

Introducing two people / Zwei Leute sich gegenseitig vorstellen

- Please join us. Have you two met? — Kommen Sie doch zu uns!
- Martha, this is Mike. Mike, this is Martha.
- Do you know each other? By the way, this is ... — Kennen Sie sich bereits?
- Let me introduce you. Sue, this is Shawn, and Shawn ... — Darf ich vorstellen?
- May I introduce you to Mrs. Lewis, our press attaché? — Darf ich Sie ... vorstellen?
- I'd like you to meet Mr. Kenton, the head of the department. — Darf ich Sie bekannt machen mit

Meeting someone you haven't seen for a while / Jemanden treffen, den Sie schon eine Weile nicht gesehen haben

- Oh my God! Is that you? How have you been? – Fine, thanks. How about you? – Not too bad, business as usual. — Sind Sie das? / Bist Du das?
- Hi, it's good to see you.
- What are you up to? Still at the bank? — Was machst Du so?

Meeting an old acquaintance / Einen alten Bekannten wiedererkennen

– Excuse me, are you Mike? Mike Miller, electric appliances? Didn't we meet at the trade fair last June?	
– I beg your pardon, you're not by any chance...	zufällig
– Have we met before?	
– You look familiar!	bekannt, vertraut
– Fancy meeting you here!	Nanu, du hier?

A person meeting old friends in a group / Wie eine Einzelperson eine bekannte Gruppe begrüßt

– How's everybody?	Wie geht es euch?
– Hello everyone. It's good to see you all.	
– Hi gang. I haven't seen you for a while. Where have you been? How come we haven't seen each other for such a long time?	Hallo Leute! (sehr informell)
– How have you been?	Was treibst Du so?

How a person introduces himself or herself to a group / Wie ein Einzelner sich einer Gruppe vorstellt

– Is this the group from the Motor Company? I've heard much about you.	
– (Do you) mind if I join you?	Was dagegen, wenn ich mich anschließe?

– If I may introduce myself. My name is ...	Ich möchte mich vorstellen.

How a group meets a foreign person / Wie eine Gruppe eine neue Person trifft

– Have we met before? My name is...	Kennen wir uns?
– You don't look familiar. I'm Steve, what's your name?	
– Are you new around here? Welcome to...	Sind Sie neu hier?
– Is this your first time here? Nice to meet you.	

Typical start-up phrases / Typische Konversationsanfänge

– It's a beautiful day, isn't it?	
– Another Monday, back to work.	Schon wieder Montag, an die Arbeit.
– Good morning. How are you today?	
– How is everybody?	
– Are you from this area?	Sind Sie von hier?
– I'm from here. In fact, my family has lived here for the last two centuries.	
– I've heard much about this city. It is well known for its many cultural activities. Do you agree?	

Typical ending phrases / Typisches Ende der Konversation

- Have a nice day.
- See you later / next week / in the afternoon.
- Enjoy your day. — Einen schönen Tag.
- Talk to you soon. — Bis bald.

Receptions und Conferences / Empfänge und Tagungen

In vielen Ländern ist es üblich, sich zu Stehempfängen oder einem Umtrunk zu treffen, um Neuankömmlinge vorzustellen, um sich informell über geschäftliche Ereignisse zu informieren oder einfach um die so genannten „weichen" Faktoren des Geschäftslebens zu pflegen. Entweder werden Sie formell zu diesen kleinen Stehempfängen eingeladen oder Sie werden nebenbei darüber unterrichtet, dass eine derartige reception (Empfang) stattfindet. Natürlich wird damit von Ihnen erwartet, ebenfalls dort zu erscheinen. Bei Kongressen und Tagungen gehört eine reception (hier: Stehempfang) zum cultural package (Kulturpaket). Bei der Anmeldung bekommen Sie in der Regel eine kleine Mappe, die das Programm, Informationen über den Tagungsort sowie Ihr Namensschild beinhaltet. Meist wird auch noch Ihre Arbeitsstätte, Ihre Universität oder Ihr research institute (Forschungsinstitut) dazu geschrieben. Dieses Schild sollten Sie sich sofort anstecken, es erleichtert die Kommunikation und die Anrede für die anderen enorm.

In den USA fängt eine Konferenz meist mit einer plenary welcoming session – einer Vollversammlung zum Zweck der Begrüßung – an, so dass sich der erste Stehempfang gleich danach anschließt. Mit einem Getränk und etwas finger food, pretzels (AmE Salzstangen) oder ein paar munchies (Knabberzeug) begeben Sie sich nun unter die Menge, die sich Richtung Bar immer dichter drängt. Dies sind perfekte Bedingungen, um seinen Small Talk anzufangen.

Example

Jo: Oh, I'm so glad that they serve some food here. My flight was delayed and I haven't eaten all day. By the way, I'm Jo.	ich bin froh, dass; übrigens
Sally: Hi Jo, how are you? I see you're from the University of Wisconsin. Are you at the Madison campus, or further north?	
Jo: I'm at the Madison campus. Have you been there?	
Sally: As a matter of fact, I have. I did my **undergraduate** work there.	in der Tat
Jo: Really! It's a small world, isn't it? Did you like it in Madison?	Wie klein ist doch die Welt!
Sally: Yes, I did, very much indeed. I loved being near the lake and people were so kind.	die Leute waren sehr freundlich
Jo: And your name tag says Arizona. You are now in Arizona?	auf Ihrem Namensschild lese ich
Sally: Yes, I am. I just moved there six months ago. It sure takes a while to get used to the heat.	Es braucht seine Zeit
Jo: I bet it does. I've never been there, but I'd love to see the Grand Canyon one day. Well, it was nice talking to you. Enjoy the conference.	Das glaube ich Ihnen.
Sally: Thank you, you too.	

Useful phrases

At receptions / Bei Empfängen

- Is this your first conference?
- It's an interesting party. – Yes it is, isn't it?
- It's nice to get a few colleagues together for a drink!
- You're from South America, aren't you?
- Yes, I'm from Colombia. And you, where are you from?
- Sorry, I didn't catch your name. – It's Joyce. Joyce Pine. — verstehen, 'mitkriegen'
- Do you fancy another drink? – Yes, please. I'll have a Scotch. — mögen, gern haben
- Which hotel are you staying in? – The Mariott. It's just around the corner. — gleich um die Ecke
- Can I give you a lift back to your hotel? — mitnehmen (im Auto);
- That's very kind of you but there is a shuttle service running every 15 minutes. — Pendelverkehr

Get-togethers that serve food / Empfänge, die auch etwas zum Essen anbieten

- This buffet looks wonderful!
- The food tastes delicious.
- Have you tried the chicken wings yet? They're very tasty. — Haben Sie schon ... probiert?
- I guess I'll try some of the fried onion rings. They smell so good. — (AmE) Ich glaube

Invitations / Einladungen

Eine Einladung nach Hause ist, ebenso wie in Deutschland, als ein Fortschritt in den Beziehungen zu sehen, als Beginn einer Freundschaft, die über das Geschäftliche hinausgehen kann. Eine Einladung nach Hause kann auf verschiedene Weisen geschehen. Mündliche Einladungen sind oft schwer zu deuten. Wie oft hat nicht schon jemand zu Ihnen gesagt It would be so nice to have you over one day oder Let's get together. Give me a call, will you? Und dann passierte gar nichts! Haben Sie vielleicht die indirekte Einladung nicht verstanden? Why don't you oder Would you like to nehmen hierbei Sonderstellungen ein: Diese Indirektheit ist ein Zeichen der Höflichkeit und bedeutet in etwa „Möchten Sie". Die Einladung ist damit folglich ausgesprochen. Sie können nach einem Would you like to come by? gleich einen Termin für Ihren Besuch ausmachen.

Es kann aber auch ein Anruf sein: Sue, would you like to spontaneously join us for dinner, tonight? Oder es wird Ihnen eine kleine Notiz gemailt: Please join us for a BBQ on Saturday afternoon at the old pier. Formeller ist eine schriftliche Einladung.

Example

Dear Sue
Would you and your partner like to join us for dinner this coming Sunday at five o'clock? We look forward to seeing you then.
Sincerely,
Cindy and her family

würdest du mit deinem Freund zum Essen kommen

Nach einer derartigen Einladung sollte sich Sue bei Cindy melden, sich für die Einladung bedanken und Ihr Kommen telefonisch, schriftlich oder per E-Mail bestätigen.

Example

Dear Cindy, thank you so very much for the invitation. We'd love to come. See you on Sunday at five o'clock. Sue.

Wird zu einer Party mit vielen Gästen gebeten, wird häufig ein potluck organisiert, d.h. jeder Gast bringt eine Kleinigkeit zum Essen oder Trinken mit.

Example

Rebecca and her partner John have invited their neighbors for a potluck dinner. Judy, their next-door neighbor, is the first to ring the doorbell.

Judy: Hi! I hope I'm not too early. *(Hoffentlich bin ich nicht zu früh dran)*

John: No, please come in. Welcome to our home.

Judy: Thanks for the invitation. *(Danke für die Einladung)* I brought some fruit salad. Maybe we should *(Vielleicht sollten wir besser ...)* put it in the fridge.

John: Sure, no problem. Please follow me to the kitchen.

Judy: You have a lovely home.

John: Thank you. Would you like to get *(Hätten Sie gerne)* a tour of the house?

Rebecca: Hello Judy! Welcome. It's so good to see you here. *(Schön, dass du da bist!)*

Oh, you brought a fruit salad. Yummy! *(Lecker!)* That sure looks good.

Useful phrases

Invitations / Einladungen

- Would you and your partner like to come over for dinner on Friday?

- You are cordially invited to join us for a little get-together this coming Sunday at 5 o'clock. — herzlich
- Why don't you spend the weekend with us in our cabin near the lake? — Möchest Du / Möchten Sie
- My family would like to get to know you. Would you like to come over for Sunday brunch? — herüber kommen, vorbei kommen
- Would you like to hit some tennis balls right after work on Friday? — gleich nach
- What are you doing on Friday night? Shall we go and watch a movie?

Accepting invitations / Einladungen annehmen

- Thank you so very much. I'd love to come.
- Thanks a lot. That is very sweet of you. — sehr nett von Ihnen
- Sounds like a great idea. What would you like me to bring along? — Das klingt gut!
- Thank you. I'd be delighted to meet the rest of your family. — sehr erfreut
- Oh, that's so kind of you. Yes, I could come and visit you this weekend. — liebenswürdig

Declining invitations / Einladungen ablehnen

- Thank you. I'd love to come, but I already have other engagements. — Verpflichtungen

- Thank you so very much, but I'm afraid I can't make it. — bedauere, ich bin leider verhindert
- That is awfully kind of you, but I'm out of town as of Thursday. — ausgesprochen nett
- Oh no! That sounds like a wonderful idea, but I'm going to visit my in-laws this coming weekend. — Schwiegereltern

Reactions on declining invitations / Reaktionen auf eine Ablehnung

- We would love to have you over. Maybe some other time. — bei uns haben
- That's too bad. Let's shoot for the following weekend? — anpeilen
- Let's try it another time. Just let me know what fits your schedule. — (BE) timetable
- Never mind. We'll work it out at a later time. — Das macht nichts.

Arriving at the home / Ankunft im Haus der Gastgeber

- Here we are! Thanks for the invitation. — Da sind wir!
- We made it. You sure gave good instructions for getting to your place. — Anleitungen
- This is a lovely home.
- What a beautiful home you have!
- Oh, isn't that beautiful! I like the way you remodelled the porch (AmE). How did you do that? — (BE) veranda

Host welcoming guests / Begrüßung durch den Gastgeber

- Welcome. Feel at home. — Fühlen Sie sich wie zuhause.
- Good evening. Make yourself comfortable. — Machen Sie es sich gemütlich.
- It's so good to see you. Welcome to our home. — Es ist schön Sie zu sehen.
- Please come on in. It's so great to have you here. — Bitte kommen Sie doch herein.

Complimenting food / Komplimente fürs Essen

- This food tastes wonderful.
- This is absolutely delicious. The meat is so tender. What butcher do you go to? — ausgesprochen köstlich
- I didn't know that you're such a good cook.
- I love the mixture of vegetables and spices in your soup. Is this a secret recipe or may I have it?
- May I have some more of the fruit dessert? It's irresistible. — Kann ich bitte noch etwas ... haben?
- Thank you for the tasty meal. — schmackhaft

Comments on the home and garden / Kommentare zu Haus und Garten

- You have such a marvellous home.

- I adore the way you decorated your living room. — bewundern
- I'll take a good look at your splendid garden. — sich etwas genau ansehen
- How long have you been living in this beautiful old apartment (AmE)? — (BE) flat
- Please tell me, what do I need to do to have such a well-tended garden?
- Did you build everything on your own? It looks very nice.
- You live in a historic neighborhood. Do many people renovate and restore their homes? — renovieren; restaurieren
- I was told that this is a very dynamic neighborhood. Do you agree? — Stimmt das?

Saying Goodbye / Verabschiedung

So schön Einladungen und Treffen auch sein mögen und so schön es sich anfühlt, integriert zu werden, alles muss einmal zu Ende gehen. Sollte Ihre Gastgeberin öfters auf die Uhr schauen oder anfangen zu gähnen, dann wäre es vielleicht an der Zeit, auch müde zu erscheinen und sich schnell zu verabschieden: Oops, all of a sudden, I'm so tired. If I may excuse myself and go home. Auch beim Verabschieden sollten Sie sich „Small Talk"-getreu äußern.

Example

Guest: What a wonderful evening. You're such great hosts. Thank you so much for having me. This was one of the best meals I've had for a long time. — großartige Gastgeber; für die Einladung

Host: You're welcome anytime. I'm so glad you could make it and we finally met. We should do this more often. — jeder Zeit herzlich willkommen; ich bin so froh, dass Sie kommen konnten

Guest: That sounds like a good idea. So the next time I would like to invite you to my home. Are you interested in sports?

Host: Yes, I am.

Guest: Good! I just bought a large TV screen and it sure is great for watching the basketball games. But now, I'm afraid I should head for home. As you know, I've a long way to drive. Thanks again for having me. Bye now. — auf den Weg machen; nochmals vielen Dank

Host: Drive safely!

Useful phrases

Guest saying goodbye / Der Gast verabschiedet sich

- Thank you so much. I'm afraid I should go now. — Leider muss ich gehen!
- You're wonderful hosts. Thanks for having me. I think I should get going now. — ich sollte jetzt besser gehen
- I wish I could stay longer, but I really should go home now. I've had a long day. — Ich würde gerne länger bleiben, doch...
- Thanks again for everything. I hate to leave but I promised the babysitter to be home by midnight. — Ich gehe ungern

Host responses / Antworten des Gastgebers

- Thanks for coming. We're so glad you could make it.
- It was a pleasure having you. — ein Vergnügen
- We enjoyed having you. Please come again.
- You are welcome any time. It is always good seeing you. — jederzeit willkommen
- It's a pity that you must go. I thought we might want to watch the basketball game together on TV. — Schade, dass...

Eating Out / Essen gehen

Fast jeder kennt den berühmten englischen Film "Dinner for one". Dieser Film ist ein klassisches Beispiel für gelungenen Small Talk beim und über das Essen: „I'm particularly fond of (ich mag besonders gerne) mulligatawny soup, James!" Ganz so geläufig müssen Sie sich nicht präsentieren, wenn Sie selbst essen gehen, doch die künstlerischen Fähigkeiten, die notwendig sind, um gleichzeitig zu essen und angenehm zu plaudern, können Sie lernen. To eat out gehört sowohl in den USA als auch in vielen europäischen Ländern viel mehr zum Lebensstil als bei uns. Reservieren Sie deshalb unbedingt frühzeitig Ihren Tisch und informieren Sie Ihre Gäste darüber: I made a reservation at the Lucky Chinese! Sonst ist das beste Restaurant am Platz (the best restaurant in town) bis auf den letzten Platz gefüllt (filled to capacity), wenn Sie ankommen. Gerade Friday night muss man häufig in den Restaurants Schlange stehen, da der Freitagabend auch die traditionelle Zeit für ein date ist.

Example

Liz and Sue are waiting to be seated at their favorite Italian restaurant. They are sitting in the lounge and are waiting to be called. (warten auf ihren Tisch)

Liz: This has always been a popular place to eat. But now that there has been a change of owners it's even more popular. You have no chance without reservations. Let's hope that they continue their fast service. I'm starving. (hoffentlich; Hunger haben)

Sue: What I heard about this place is that their menu not only serves an incredible variety of food but also includes exclusiveness. There's no other place in town that serves such authentic Italian pasta, not to mention their selection of wines. (geschweige denn)

Liz: Yes, just look around. This place is jam-packed. I sure hope we don't have to wait too long. So tell me, what else is happening in your life? (proppenvoll; was passiert bei Dir so alles)

Useful phrases

Waiting for the food / Beim Warten auf das Essen

- How have you been? — Wie geht's Dir so?
- How are you doing these days?
- What's new? Tell me all about it. — Was gibt's Neues?
- The menu looks really good.
- They offer an incredible selection of food.
- What can you recommend? Is there anything you're particularly fond of? — empfehlen; etwas ganz besonders mögen

– This is a nice place. Have you eaten here before?

Eating / Beim Essen

– How is your food? – Everything is just fine. How about yours? — Wie ist dein/ihr (Essen)?

– Do you like your meat? — (BE) joint of beef

– This tastes so good.

– I just love the wide selection of their salad buffet. I think I'll have a second serving. — sehr mögen; Nachschlag

– They always come up with new ideas for their side dishes. I just love it. — Beilagen

– This was a good choice. I like it here. — gute Wahl

– This is a lovely place to eat. Everything is just tasty and delicious.

Requests and complaints / Bitten und Beschwerden

– Excuse me please, could I have some more water? — ich hätte gern ...

– I'm afraid there is a little problem. The steak is well-done and I had ordered medium.

– Are there any specials today? For example, a soup and salad combo? — kombiniertes Angebot aus Suppe und Salat

– What can you recommend for a starter and for the main course? — Was empfehlen Sie?

– Waiter / waitress, can I have the check (AmE) / please? What do I owe you?	Rechnung, (BE) bill
– Could I please have a doggy bag?	Tüte für Reste

Finishing eating / Das Essen beenden

– I think I ate too much, but it was so good.	
– I'm afraid I've had enough. The size of their portions is incredible.	
– There is no way I can finish my dessert.	Ich kann unmöglich ...
– I really enjoyed this dinner very much. Unfortunately, I am getting tired and should hit the road.	sich auf den Heimweg machen
– Let's get the bill. It is on me, okay?	geht auf meine Rechnung
– No, I'll see to that!	ich zahle
– No, no, I'll pay for that, leave that to me!	
– I had a stressful day today, a typically heavy-going afternoon, I'd better get home.	anstrengend; hart
– I don't mean to be impolite, but I'm not feeling too well and should go home.	möchte nicht unhöflich scheinen
– This was wonderful. I hate to tell you but I need to get going.	Ich bedauere, Ihnen sagen zu müssen
– If you don't mind, I'd like to go home now.	Wenn es Ihnen recht ist

Kulturelle und sprachliche Tipps

Beim Begrüßen

Während bei Begrüßungen und Vorstellungen in der deutschen Kultur die Nachnamen und oft auch die Titel wichtig sind, bevorzugt die englisch sprechende Kultur nur die Vornamen. I'm Jo, nice to meet you. Oder, I'm Sarah. Pleased to meet you. Die Begrüßungsformel How do you do? benützt man, wenn man jemanden zum ersten Mal trifft. Als Antwort sagt man dann entweder How do you do?, wobei das you betont ist, oder I'm fine, thank you. How are you? Als unausgesprochene Regel gilt: Erzählen Sie auf diese Frage hin nicht, wie schlecht es Ihnen eventuell geht oder mit welchen schwierigen Aufgaben Sie momentan zu kämpfen haben. How are you doing? oder How is it going? sind informeller und signalisieren, dass sich die Personen schon kennen. Man sagt auch Welcome to... und nicht Welcome in .... Im britischen Englisch hört man auch Fancy seeing you again oder für Thank you auch Cheers. Sollten Sie Grüße von jemanden überbringen, der nicht anwesend sein kann, sagen Sie he/she sends his/her regards. Wenn Sie umgekehrt jemanden grüßen lassen, bitten Sie give him/her my regards oder vertraulicher say hello to him/her from me.

Formlose Treffen

In der Regel sind social gatherings zeitlich begrenzt. Deswegen sollte man sich nicht in komplexe Gesprächsthemen vertiefen, die einen die Zeit vergessen lassen. Das wäre der schnellste Weg, als Deutsche oder Deutscher beim Argumentieren und Philosophieren ertappt und erkannt zu werden. Ahmen Sie die Vorliebe der Engländer und Amerikaner nach: ein Wörtchen da, ein Sätzchen dort, eine eher belanglose Plauderei mit den Nachbarn am Buffet. Grundregel: Lieber ein How do you do? oder Nice to meet you! zu viel als eines zu wenig.

Wenn Sie sich mit Leuten länger unterhalten und dabei herausfinden, dass Sie gemeinsame Interessen haben oder eventuell geschäftlich in Verbindung treten wollen, dann können Sie ihnen ohne großes Aufhebens Ihre Visitenkarte geben. Here is my card. Give me a call when you have a chance.

Einladungen

Einladungen werden oft mit einer indirekten Einleitung formuliert: Would you oder Why don't you, die als Höflichkeit zu interpretieren ist. Sollten Sie mit einer schriftlichen Einladung zu jemandem nach Hause eingeladen worden sein, dann lesen Sie in der letzten Zeile vielleicht die Abkürzung RSVP, aus dem Französischen répondez s'il vous plaît, um Antwort wird gebeten. We gladly accept your invitation and look forward to seeing you then wäre eine mögliche Reaktion darauf. Oder This is to confirm our coming on ... Beides wären sehr formelle Antworten. Weniger formell wären zum Beispiel: Thanks for the invitation. Yes, we can make it. See you then. Oder Thank you so much. We're happy to join you for dinner then.

Gastgeschenke

Eine Einladung nach Hause ist ein Zeichen, dass man daran interessiert ist, Sie näher kennen zu lernen. Wie bei uns ist es angeraten, host und hostess zu dieser Einladung ein kleines Gastgeschenk mitzubringen. A bunch of flowers oder a bouquet sind nie verkehrt. Bei Wein hingegen kann es ungewollt zu Problemen kommen, wenn Sie Ihre Gastgeber noch nicht gut kennen. Die amerikanische Gesetzgebung trennt zwischen state und church, d.h. über Religion wird selten öffentlich geredet. So wissen Sie vielleicht gar nicht, welche Rolle Religion im Leben ihres Gastgebers spielt. Moslems trinken keinen Alkohol.

Essensgewohnheiten

Sollten Sie der Gastgeber sein und zum Essen etwas typisch Deutsches mit Schweinefleisch vorbereiten, kann auch dies zu Problemen führen. Zum einen, wenn Ihre Gäste jüdischer Herkunft sind, zum anderen wenn sie vegetarians sind oder aus gesundheitlichen Gründen eine special diet leben, beispielsweise low cholesterol oder no salt. Um solche Missverständnisse zu vermeiden, ist es üblich, Gäste bei der Einladung nach besonderen Einschränkungen bezüglich ihres Essens und Trinkens zu fragen. Please let us know any dietary restrictions you might have. Sollten Sie selbst eine Diät befolgen müssen, informieren Sie Ihre Gastgeber rechtzeitig dahingehend: I don't want to put you to any trouble, but I'm on a special diet. Aller Wahrscheinlichkeit nach bekommen Sie die gastfreundliche (hospitable) Antwort zu hören: This is no trouble at all – das ist nicht der Rede wert.

Andere Länder, andere Sitten

Bei informelleren Einladungen zu Hause ist es in den USA, ähnlich wie in Italien oder Spanien, durchaus möglich, dass der Fernseher und das Radio bei Ankunft des Besuches nicht ausgeschaltet werden. Dies ist für viele von uns gewöhnungsbedürftig, doch hat es nichts mit Unhöflichkeit zu tun. In vielen amerikanischen Haushalten ist es üblich – that's perfectly normal – dass die verschiedenen Hausbewohner ihren eigenen Fernseher haben und mehrere Geräte gleichzeitig laufen, auch das im Badezimmer.

Amerikanische Gastgeber haben in der Regel auch nichts dagegen, wenn ihre Gäste in die Küche kommen. Bei ganz ungezwungenen Zusammentreffen wird oft sogar erwartet, dass die Gäste sich selbst mit Nachschub aus dem Kühlschrank versorgen: Help yourself to drinks. They are either in the refrigerator or in the big cooler in the garden, next to the grill. Diese Aufforderungen bieten jeweils eine gute Gelegenheit, noch einmal das schöne Haus, den Garten oder die Ausstattung zu bewundern: You've put a lot of hard work into remodelling your home. Trust me, it sure shows. Jeder Gastgeber freut sich, wenn Sie seine baulichen Anstrengungen nicht nur wahrnehmen – I can't believe how much the larger windows have changed the brightness in your home – sondern auch genießen: It's so cosy. I'm very impressed how you use every corner and space in your home.

In England sieht es etwas anders aus. Als Gastgeber würde man weder Fernsehen noch Radio laufen lassen, denn dies würde als unfreundlich empfunden werden. Hier ist es ein must, ein „soziales Muss", etwa 15 Minuten zu spät zu kommen. Eine allgemeine Tendenz des britischen Small Talk ist es, sich in Untertreibungen zu äußern. I'm doing alright kann es selbst dann heißen, wenn Ihr Gastgeber vor einer großen und schwierigen Operation steht. Wenn eine britische Gastgeberin murmelt, sie sei just a little tired, sollten Sie sich schnell verabschieden, denn die Dame ist todmüde und kurz vor dem Umfallen.

In der Regel fühlen wir Deutschen uns wohl, wenn unsere Gäste lange bleiben und bis in die frühen Morgenstunden angeregt plaudern. In den USA jedoch ist dieses Verhalten erst nach längerer Bekanntschaft angebracht. Bei Ihrem ersten Besuch sollten Sie nicht allzu lange bleiben. Wenn Ihnen nach dem Nachtisch noch eine Tasse Kaffee angeboten wird, sollten Sie diese in aller Ruhe austrinken, sich dann aber zügig verabschieden.

Thank you

Nach der Einladung „Danke schön" zu sagen, ist in der englisch sprechenden Welt viel wichtiger als in Deutschland . Es ist durchaus üblich, dem Gastgeber am nächsten Tag eine Thank you note zu schicken: This is just a little note to thank you very much again for the wonderful dinner. We enjoyed it very much. Thanks again. Es gibt zu diesem Zweck auch eine Vielzahl vorgedruckter Karten. Eine weitere Variation wäre ein Anruf oder auch eine E-Mail mit kurzen Dankesworten und dem Hinweis auf eine spätere Gegeneinladung bei Ihnen:

Example
Dear Mike and Judy, thanks so much for the great dinner. You're a terrific cook, Judy. Sandra and I look forward to welcoming you both at our new home. I'll keep you posted. David.

Eating out

In Amerika ist es, anders als in Europa, nicht üblich, sich nach dem Essen im Restaurant noch weiter gemütlich zu unterhalten. Die Bedienung wird dann immer öfter an Ihren Tisch kommen mit der Frage Can I get you anything? oder sogar ungebeten die Rechnung vorbeibringen. Wenn jemand dann die Rechnung zu sich nimmt und sagt: (It's) my treat oder I'll take care of it oder it's on me today, dann sind Sie eingeladen. Wollen Sie jedoch vereinbaren, dass jeder für sich zahlt, dann sagen Sie: let's go Dutch.

In den meisten Ländern ist das Trinkgeld nicht automatisch im Preis der Speisen mit inbegriffen. Waren Service und Essen in Ordnung, dann gibt man 10-15 % der Rechnung als Trinkgeld. In den USA darf dieser tip auch mal 20 % und mehr ausmachen, wenn der Service ausnehmend gut war.

Ist von dem guten Essen noch etwas übrig, dann darf man den Ober gerne um ein doggy bag bitten: The food was excellent but a little bit too much for me. Do you happen to have a doggy bag for me? Ihr Essen wird dann eingepackt und Sie können es nach Hause mitnehmen. Ein guter Kellner wird Sie eventuell auch auf die Möglichkeit ansprechen, den

Rest Ihres Essens mitzunehmen: Would you like me to pack the rest of the food for you? oder I'll wrap the food for you. Ob der Inhalt dann wirklich für den Hund ist oder für Sie eine weitere leckere Mahlzeit ergibt, bleibt Ihr Geheimnis.

Falsche Freunde

Als falsche Freunde sollen im Folgenden diejenigen Wörter enttarnt werden, die im Englischen und Deutschen beinahe gleich geschrieben werden, aber nicht die gleiche Bedeutung haben. Lassen Sie deshalb Vorsicht bei direkten Übersetzungen walten und achten Sie darauf, das Wort im richtigen kulturellen und sozialen Kontext anzuwenden.

Das Wort date wird hierzulande für jede Art von informellen Treffen benutzt, im Englischen aber kann es eine ganz besondere Bedeutung bekommen: Lädt Jim Mary an einem Freitag Abend zu einem date (Verabredung) ein, z.B. mit der Frage What are you doing Friday night? oder Shall we go to the movies? oder I'd like to take you out for dinner. How about the new Lebanese place? kann dies der Anfang einer romantischen Beziehung werden. Traditionell gehören zu einem date ein Kinobesuch und / oder ein Essen. Früher war es automatisch der Herr, der alles bezahlte, doch dies ist heute nicht immer so. Am besten stellen Sie die Zahlungsmodalitäten gleich von Anfang an klar. Den Obstfreunden sei gesagt, es kann am date auch dates, nämlich Datteln, geben.

Beim Besuch in der Wohnung eines Kollegen oder Chefs zeigt sich jeder gerne gleich beim Eintritt in den Flur beeindruckt: You have a very nice hall oder hallway. Im Britischen sagt man auch corridor. Floor aber bedeutet entweder der Fußboden oder das Stockwerk. Wenn Ihre Gastgeberin schildert, my children love to throw their baseball caps on the floor, dann werfen ihre Kinder ihre Baseballkappen auf den Boden. Heißt es, all of our children have their bedrooms on the first floor whereas we have ours on the ground floor, sind die Stockwerke gemeint: Alle unsere Kinder haben ihre Schlafzimmer im ersten Stock. Unterschiede zeigen sich hier zwischen britischem und amerikanischem Englisch: Was im Britischen der ground floor ist, ist im Amerikanischen der first floor. Ein Haus kann dadurch also größer beschrieben werden als es eigentlich ist.

Helle Zimmer werden gerne mit Komplimenten überschüttet, à la I like the way this room is particularly bright in summer – Schön, wie hell dieses Zimmer im Sommer ist. Im Englischen bedeutet das Wort hell aber das ganze Gegenteil, nämlich Hölle: As it is written, our father is in heaven and the devil in hell.

Small Talk in the Office / Small Talk im Büro

Ohne Networking kommt man heute beruflich kaum noch weiter. Aber wie fängt man das an? Mit Small Talk! Mit einer Plauderei zwischen Tür und Angel, einem Kompliment am Montagmorgen oder ein paar angeregten Sätzen im Aufzug knüpfen und pflegen Sie Beziehungen.

Conversations in the Office / Bürogespräche

Wenn Ihre Kollegin bittet, Could somebody please answer the phone for me? I'm on the other line, und Sie zugleich eine E-Mail erhalten, des Inhalts May I remind everyone that we have our usual Monday morning staff meeting in the lounge, starting in five minutes, und Ihnen dann noch Ihr Chef auf die Schulter klopft mit der Information: Your fiscal report looks really good. Just add the latest figures and have the CEO sign it, dann ist es höchste Zeit für eine Atempause – am besten mit ein wenig Small Talk. Aber nicht nur dann: Montagmorgens ist es besonders wichtig, mit seinen Kollegen und Kolleginnen zu plaudern. How was your weekend? oder Did you enjoy your weekend? gehört zu den erwarteten Standardfragen. Je nach Länge der Bekanntschaft und Vertrautheit dürfen Sie auch gerne mehr fragen: So, how was the movie? How did your daughter's softball game go?

Example

The secretaries are exchanging information about their weekend activities.

Sec 1: Did you have a nice weekend?

Sec 2: Oh yes, I did. My partner and I went up north to the mountains. The weather was just beautiful, the air crisp and clear. We enjoyed a nice and peaceful time at our log cabin. How about yourself?

Sec 1: Well, nothing special, except that we tried the new restaurant, the one kitty-corner (AmE) to the new bank subsidiary. They serve German-Austrian food. It sure tastes good, but we'd better not talk about the calorie intake.

tauschen Informationen aus

Und selbst?

nichts Besonderes

schräg gegenüber (BE) diagonally opposite; Tochtergesellschaft; reden wir lieber nicht

Useful phrases

Director to secretary / Chef zur Sekretärin

- Here we go again. Could you please update me on my appointment schedule? — Jetzt geht's wieder los.
- Have you recovered from last week's stress? — Haben Sie sich erholt
- Are you ready for another really busy and important week?
- I seem to have started on the wrong foot. How about you?

Director to staff / Chef zu den Mitarbeitern

- Good morning everybody. I hope you all had a great weekend. — Ich hoffe, Sie hatten alle ...
- Could I please have everybody's attention? — Aufmerksamkeit
- I got a call from the office of R & D (Research & Development). Their presentation will be postponed. — verschoben
- Can everybody please listen? There's been a change for our staff meeting. It will be one hour later. — Es gab eine Änderung

Asking for assistance / Um Hilfe bitten

- Could you please hand me the minutes of our last annual meeting? — Sitzungsprotokoll
- Why don't you finish the memo first — Warum beenden Sie nicht zuerst

and then finalize the job advertisement?	das... (höfliche Aufforderung)
– I need to postpone my meeting with the director of sales. Please call her and let her know.	informieren Sie sie
– Could you please assist me? I'd appreciate it if you could call Mrs. Smith for me and tell her...	Ich wäre ihnen sehr dankbar, wenn

Polite standard phrases / Höfliche Standardsätze

– I'm so sorry for the delay. We've been extremely busy.	Verzögerung
– I'm afraid Ms. Jones has stepped out of the office.	kurz nach draußen gegangen
– If there is anything else I can be of help with, please let me know.	wobei ich Ihnen helfen kann
– I need to drop something off at the post office and the bank. Can I get you anything?	Soll ich Ihnen etwas mitbringen?

Polite requests / Höfliche Aufforderungen

– May I please use your hole puncher for a moment?	Könnte ich bitte...?
– Would it be alright if I sent the interim report off tomorrow?	Wäre es in Ordnung, wenn...?
– Would you do me a favour and help me unpack the new filing cabinet?	einen Gefallen tun
– Could I ask you to attend the board of directors meeting with me?	Würde es Ihnen etwas ausmachen

– I was wondering if you might be able to design new visitor badges. — könnten Sie vielleicht

Compliments / Komplimente

– You did a really great job on that report.
– Well done. Keep up the good work! — Gut gemacht.
– Congratulations on a most interesting presentation. — Ich gratuliere zu
– Nice job on that business deal. You clearly put a lot of effort into it. — Gute Arbeit geleistet

Compliments on the looks / Komplimente für das Aussehen

– Did you get a perm? It looks nice. — Dauerwelle
– Your shoes look very comfortable and elegant.
– Did you get a hair cut? It fits you perfectly! — steht Dir ausgezeichnet
– I like your new shirt. That is a good color on you. — Diese Farbe steht Ihnen.
– That tie looks very handsome on you. — hübsch

Talking about People / Über Personen sprechen

Egal in welcher Situation Sie den Small Talk anwenden, früher oder später werden Sie auch über andere Personen sprechen müssen: Oh, Mary! She's really a nice person. She has such an outgoing personality. Vielleicht machen Sie sich Sorgen um eine Kollegin: Have you seen Eileen lately? She lost quite some weight. I hope she's doing alright. Oft müssen Sie auch einem Kollegen kurz beschreiben, wie die Person aussieht, um die sich das Gespräch gerade dreht: Remember? He's that tall blond guy, I'd say 6'4".

Example 1

JJ ("JayJay") is in his mid-forties, has a few grey hairs, and his hair is receding. He's kind of stocky and wears glasses.	Mitte 40 untersetzt

Example 2

Liz: Sue, I haven't seen you for a while. How have you been?	
Sue: Oh, I've been so busy, it's not funny.	Ich war so beschäftigt, es ist nicht mehr lustig
Did I tell you that I have a new boss? She's really nice but demanding.	nett, aber fordernd
Liz: What does she look like?	
Sue: She is petite and thin. She's got dark, curly hair. She usually wears her hair combed back, in a ponytail. Overall, her physical appearance is very neat and tidy.	insgesamt

Useful phrases

Description of hair and body / Beschreibung von Haaren und Körper

– She has wide cheeks and her hair is completely straight and thick.	
– He's bald and a giant of a man.	Riese
– She's slight and slender. She wears her hair in plaits (BE) / pigtails (AE).	zart; schlank; Zöpfe

- He's on the corpulent side and his hair's thinning. — eher beleibt
- There's nothing to her. Her wig looks very real. — lang und dürr
- For his age, he's below average height. He likes his hair combed forward and with fringes. — für sein Alter
- Her husband is rather plump. — ziemlich rundlich
- Thanks to all his workouts, he looks very muscular and he's fond of his crew cut. — Meckifrisur

People's characters / Zur Person

- You can't miss his big and friendly smile. — nicht übersehen
- She is one of those old-fashioned secretaries: straightforward and down to earth. — aufrichtig
- The perfect receptionist should be outgoing. — gesellig
- Many VIPs appear snobbish and arrogant. — scheinen
- Most CEOs are determined to get their work done. — Geschäftsleiter; (BE) Managing director
- Successful headhunters are known to be highly competitive. — bekannt für
- The new product manager seems to be very ambitious. — scheint ... zu sein
- It seems to me that the purchasing manager is very demanding. — anscheinend

- I agree that fashion designers should be imaginative. — Ich bin auch der Meinung, dass
- Opinion has it that an experienced public relations director is understanding and a chief accountant should be most reliable. — Die gängige Meinung ist; Hauptbuchhalter(in)

Being positive and complimenting / Komplimente machen

- She looks very attractive and her baby looks adorable.
- Beyond all question she is a very pretty person. — fraglos
- That's all very well, but he doesn't look very handsome. — Das ist ja schön und gut
- With all due respect, she looks amazingly young for her age. — Bei aller Hochachtung
- He is incredibly fit for his age.
- She is unbelievably talented in coaching. — unglaublich
- I believe that his presentation was extremely well received. — der Meinung sein
- Your proposal was fabulous and of the highest quality. — Vorschlag war genial
- Congratulations! You did such an excellent job. — Das war ausgezeichnet

Meeting Customers / Kunden willkommen heißen

Viele Leute beherzigen das alte Sprichwort: "Der erste Eindruck ist entscheidend". Dies gilt nicht nur für das äußerliche Erscheinungsbild, sondern auch für die Wahl der sozialen Verhaltensmuster und des richtigen Tons: How do you do? ist sehr höflich und formell und wird in der Bank oder beim lawyer bei der ersten Begrüßung verwendet. Den freundlichen butcher oder den altgedienten postal clerk wird man eher gefühlsbetont und viel informeller begrüßen mit Hi dear! How are you today? Als Antwort schallt einem dann vielleicht ein Hi honey! What can I get you today? entgegen.

Example

George is the new director of sales for one of the leading car dealers of the whole region. One of his goals is to promote international business. Thus, he arranged for a meeting with his international colleagues.

George: Good morning everybody and welcome to the headquarters of Qualitycars Germany.

Thanks for coming to our first international meeting. I hope you had a pleasant trip and that your accommodations are fine. If there is anything we can be of help with, please talk to my secretary, Sue. What I would like to do today is give you a tour of the plant, discuss our latest sales figures and then have you introduce your ideas of how we can strengthen our international marketing strategies.

Besprechung anordnen/vereinbaren
willkommen im
Vielen Dank, dass Sie gekommen sind
Unterkünfte;
Wenn wir Ihnen mit irgend etwas behilflich sein können

Useful phrases

Way to the company / Der Weg zur Firma

- Did you find us alright? – Thank you, you gave very good instructions. — gleich gefunden
- Welcome to our company. Did you have any problems finding us?
- Here you are. It's good to see you. Please sign in. — sich eintragen
- Hello everyone. So, you made it here on time in spite of the rush hour jam. — rechtzeitig; Stoßverkehr

Welcoming guests or customers / Gäste oder Kunden willkommen heißen

- Welcome to our company!
- On behalf of our company, I'd like to welcome you. — Im Namen...
- Thank you for coming to ...
- You must be our guests from France and Italy. Welcome. It's good to have you here. — Schön, dass Sie da sind
- May I take your coat? The check-room is right here. — Garderobe (BE) wardrobe
- Please take a seat. Mrs. Fine will be with you in a moment. — wird sich um Sie kümmern
- It's good to see you. Why don't you have a seat and relax a little? I'll let them know that you're here. — Setzen Sie sich doch

- Make yourself comfortable. Please help yourself to some coffee, tea and donuts. — bedienen Sie sich

Introducing the building / Räumlichkeiten vorstellen

- Here's a map of the building. You're on the 5th floor. The lounge and the restrooms are next to the elevator. — Toilette, (BE) men's/ladies' room
- You're in front of the cafeteria. Your meeting will be in the conference room, two doors down on the left-hand side. — zwei Türen weiter
- May I give you an overview of the building? Each floor has the exact same lay-out: four offices, one conference room and a lounge. — Darf ich Ihnen ... geben
- We reserved a little room for you. It's right next to the conference hall. You're welcome to leave your coats and jackets there and help yourself to snacks. — Gerne dürfen Sie ...

Meeting regular customers / Stammkunden treffen

- Hi, how have you been? – Nothing new.
- Look who's here: our dear old friend Mark. — Schau, wer da ist!
- Hello Mrs. Rice. How are you today? My boss is expecting you. Please come on in.
- Hello Larry, it's good to see you again. Tell me, how is your family? And how is business? — wie läuft es im Geschäft

Socializing Events at Work / Gesellige Treffen am Arbeitsplatz

Für viele Leute sind gesellige Treffen am Arbeitsplatz mit negativen Emotionen oder gar mit Ängsten verbunden. Was soll man bloß sagen, um sich von seiner besten Seite zu zeigen und sich ja nicht zu blamieren? Worüber reden? Und wie viel? Über diese Unsicherheit hilft Small Talk hinweg: Pure Höflichkeit verlangt es, immer etwas Nettes zu äußern, selbst wenn schwierige Themen und Zeiten anstehen. Ist der erste Schritt zur Kommunikation getan, fällt der nächste schon leichter. Vergessen Sie dabei nicht: Allen anderen fällt ihr Auftreten vor Kollegen auch nicht leichter als Ihnen.

Example

It is international advertising's annual convention. Managing partner, Jo Smith, and marketing manager, Sandra Miller, of two different companies, meet during the coffee break.

Smith: Hi Sandra, are you enjoying the conference? — gefällt Ihnen

Miller: Oh, hello Jo. Yes, I'm enjoying it. How about yourself?

Smith: So far, so good. To be honest, I can't wait to hear our guest speaker. He is supposed to be very good. People are just raving about him. — ehrlich gesagt

Miller: Yes, his work is well received. I've heard nothing but good things about him. Ah, the bell is ringing. We'd better get going and find a seat. — Wir sollten uns in Bewegung setzen

I'm pretty sure it will be packed. — ziemlich sicher

Smith: Well, let's see what we can learn. — schauen wir mal;

Why don't we meet up again after the talk? — Wie wär's, wenn

Miller: Sounds like a good idea. See you then. — Bis später

Useful phrases

Before a presentation / Vor einem Vortrag

- I can't wait to hear him/her speak. — es kaum erwarten können
- Their work is highly praised. — hochgelobt
- One hears nothing but good things about him/her. — nur Gutes hören
- Everybody likes his dry sense of humor.

After a presentation / Nach einem Vortrag

- I really enjoyed your presentation. — sehr genossen
- Job well done! Keep up the good work. — weiter so
- You hit some very interesting points.
- You did a fine job of explaining something complex in a simple way. — Sie haben das gut gemacht

During a coffee break / Während einer Kaffeepause

- Hi John. Here we go again. Another convention. — Tagung
- Are you enjoying the conference? — Tagung
- The coffee and the Danish feel good right now, don't they? — nicht wahr?
- They always do such a great job with serving hot coffee and donuts.
- Which sessions are you going to? — Sitzungen, Vorträge

- How did your presentation go? — Wie ist Ihr Vortrag verlaufen?

Welcoming a new a colleague / Einen neuen Kollegen willkommen heißen

- Well, I called for this meeting to welcome our new colleague. — einberufen
- I'd like to take this opportunity to welcome and introduce... — möchte diese Gelegenheit nutzen um...
- This is Karen Reilly. Welcome on board. — Willkommen bei uns.
- I'm absolutely delighted to have Mike Wood as our new data processing manager. — ich bin höchst erfreut

Get-togethers at work / Treffen am Arbeitsplatz

- On behalf of our company, I would like to welcome you to ... — heiße ich Sie willkommen bei
- It's good to see you all here.
- First of all, I would like to thank Jill for taking care of the food and drinks.
- I'd like to take this opportunity to thank all of you for ... — Gelegenheit ergreifen
- Help yourself to something to drink and eat. It's on the house. — Es geht aufs Haus.

Meeting colleagues at the cafeteria / Kollegen/innen, die Sie in der Kantine treffen

- May I join you?
- Is this seat taken already? — Ist hier noch frei?
- Hello Bob, please have a seat.
- Why don't you join us? Then we can talk a little bit. — Kommen Sie doch zu uns!
- Oh Barb, I'm glad to see you. Can I sit with you? — Kann ich mich zu Euch setzen?
- So, how've you been?
- The food isn't too bad, is it?
- How is business for you? — Wie läuft es geschäftlich?
- Did you watch the game yesterday?
- Congratulations! I heard you got promoted. — befördert
- It is my great pleasure to welcome Judy White to our firm. — Es ist mir eine große Freude

Parties, Anniversaries, and other Events / Parties, Geburtstage und andere Treffen

In den USA ist es Gang und Gäbe, für langjährige Arbeitskollegen/innen eine surprise party zu organisieren. Meist erfolgt hierfür eine schriftliche Einladung an die gesamte Abteilung, mit der Bitte um strikte Geheimhaltung, so dass die Überraschung auch gut geplant ist und gelingt. Auch die

Anerkennung durch eine Abschiedsfeier ist ein wichtiges geschäftliches Ritual.

Festtage auch am Arbeitsplatz zu feiern, ist in den USA beliebter als in Deutschland. Das mag damit zusammen hängen, dass es in Deutschland weit mehr gesetzliche Feiertage gibt als in den USA oder in Großbritannien. Neben den Geburtstagen, denen am Arbeitsplatz mit einem kleinen get-together, einem zwanglosen Treffen gedacht wird, gehören dazu der secretaries day am 21. April sowie offizielle Feiertage, wie z.B. Weihnachten oder Ostern.

Example

Dear colleagues,
as you might know, Nancy is celebrating her 25th anniversary at this company in May. Thus, we would like to organize a little surprise party for her on May 1. We thought we'd do a potluck. Please mark on the list what you'd like to bring. We also bought her a little present for her Hummel collection. We got her the little flower girl. It would be nice if each of you could contribute five dollars.
Please see Joan for details. Hope to see you there.
The party committee, Ann & Amy.

wie ihr vielleicht wißt

Wir dachten, jeder bringt etwas mit

Es wäre schön, wenn ... beitragen; Weitere Einzelheiten bitte mit Joan klären

Useful Phrases

At the (surprise) party / Auf der (Überraschungs)party

– Surprise, surprise. I can't believe we managed to keep it secret, but here it is.

Ich hätte nicht gedacht

- I can't believe this. You really hit me by surprise. — völlig überrascht
- You made my day. Thank you all so very much. — den Tag „gerettet"
- This is very special to me. You're so sweet. — bedeutet mir viel
- I don't know what to say, but it sure means a lot to me.
- We wouldn't know how the office could exist without you.
- Well Nancy, we thought that you, the pearl of our office, deserve a surprise party. — die Perle unseres Büros

Farewell parties / Verabschiedungen

- On behalf of all of us, we'd like to thank you for your hard work. — im Namen aller
- We hate to see you leave but wish you the very best in your new job. — das Beste wünschen
- We'll miss you but are delighted to know that you were transferred to the company's site in Europe. — erfreut, entzückt
- It's time to say goodbye to you, Jack, and thank you for your commitment to excellence in all those years. Best of luck. — Einsatz, Engagement

- Congratulations on your new job. We understand that this will be a big step forward in your career. All the best and keep in touch. — in Kontakt bleiben
- We'll miss you but are delighted to know that you were transferred to the company's site in Europe. — freuen uns zu wissen
- Thank you so much for everything. Best of luck in whatever you do. — alles erdenklich Gute!

Anniversaries, jubilees / Jubiläen

- Today it's Vivian's 20th work anniversary. Thank you for all the good work.
- On behalf of all of us, a big thank you for 15 years of dedicated service to our company. — Im Namen aller
- Manuel, it's hard to believe that you have been with us for 25 years. You're the soul of this office. Congratulations and thank you so much. — Es ist kaum zu glauben
- It is my great pleasure to honor Rick for 30 years of excellence and hard work here in our office. — (BE) to honour; ehren

Birthdays / Geburtstage

- Happy birthday to you. Lots of happiness and peace.
- Have a wonderful birthday.

- We wish you a happy birthday and all the best in whatever you do. — das Beste in all Ihren Unternehmungen
- Happy birthday. May all your dreams come true.

Secretaries day / Sekretärinnentag

- On this secretaries day we would like to thank all of you for your continuous support. — Unterstützung
- I'd like to take this opportunity to congratulate all of you on your outstanding work. — hervorragend
- Thank you for your hard work. You're always there when we need you. It's greatly appreciated. — hoch schätzen, würdigen
- We can't thank you enough for your efforts. — Einsatz

Christmas / Weihnachten

- Have a merry Christmas and a happy new year.
- Have a happy holiday season and all the best for the coming new year. — Frohe Festtage
- May the spirit of the season be with you throughout the new year. — die Besinnlichkeit der Feiertage
- Wishing you a merry Christmas and a prosperous new year. — gedeihlich, erfolgreich

Get-togethers at work / Gesellige Treffen am Arbeitsplatz

- Enjoy the get-together and relax a little bit. — Beisammensein
- Let's take a break and chat a little bit. — Pause machen
- Make one of the party, Fred, enjoy the munchies and punch! — Schließ dich an
- For a change we'll be meeting in Bridget´s office. — zur Abwechslung;
- You need a change, Francis, help yourself to something to drink and eat. It's on the house. — Sie müssen mal ausspannen

Kulturelle und sprachliche Tipps

Komplimente

Wie die Beispiele zeigen, kann Small Talk im Büro aus vielen kleinen und verschiedenen Dingen bestehen. Es muss nicht viel Aufhebens gemacht werden, jedoch gibt es immer etwas, das man mit einem kleinen Kompliment erwähnen kann: I really like your new blouse. Doch bitte seien Sie vorsichtig, wenn Sie jemanden beschreiben und dabei umgangssprachliche Floskeln benutzen. Diese können sehr verletzend wirken. Vermeiden Sie Ausdrücke wie skinny, like a pipe cleaner, like a lamp-post, puny, wenn Sie eine sehr dünne Person beschreiben, und built like a barrel oder obese, wenn die Person übergewichtig ist. Sachliche Begriffe wären in solchen Fällen thin und big.

Im Englischen gilt es als sehr unhöflich auf Komplimente nicht mit irgendeiner Form des Thank you oder weiteren Kommentaren zu reagieren.

Example
Liz: Did you get a new sweater? It looks very nice.
Libby: Thank you. My husband got it for me for our wedding anniversary.

Egal wie viel wichtige geschäftliche Dinge zu besprechen sind, es ist immer genug Zeit, um eine neue Frisur, ein neues Kleidungsstück oder das neue Blumengesteck auf dem Schreibtisch anerkennend zu erwähnen. Je besser Sie eine Person kennen, desto ausführlicher können Sie dabei werden.

Sollten Sie derselben Person am gleichen Tag schon zum dritten Mal auf dem Gang begegnen, dann wäre ein how are you? im Vorbeigehen nicht mehr ausreichend. Es wäre eher an der Zeit, kurz stehen zu bleiben und noch etwas zu kommentieren. Sei es die Hektik des heutigen Tages It's another hectic day oder It's one of those days oder seien es die Resultate des regionalen Sportvereins: Did you hear? Our football team won again!

Höflichkeit

Was für viele Deutsche auch ungewohnt sein kann, ist die äußerst höfliche Formulierung von Bitten und Anforderungen. Would you please (Würden Sie bitte) zählt hierbei zu den wichtigsten Wendungen. Can you oder could you please oder may I ask you to do this sind ebenfalls höflich, doch would ist noch eine Spur höflicher. Ein verbaler Missgriff, ein no-no (Tabu), wäre die sehr wörtliche und direkte Formulierung: I want you to do this right now! Dies kommt im Englischen einem Befehl gleich und sollte auch nur als solcher angewandt werden. Sagt Ihr Chef freundlich zu Ihnen: Why don't you work on the invoice right now and finish the inventory later? dann heißt das nicht, dass Sie hier die Qual der Wahl zwischen Rechnungsstellung und Bestandsaufnahme haben, sondern dass Sie schleunigst die Rechnung schreiben.

Social Events im Büro

Neben Geburtstagsfeiern oder Jubiläen sind die Neueinstellung eines Mitarbeiters oder public holidays (gesetzliche Feiertage) weitere social events im Büro sein. Dabei wird vorher abgesprochen, welcher Kollege den Kuchen oder die cookies (BE biscuits) mitbringt oder welche Kollegin die Glückwunschkarte kauft, die dann von allen unterschrieben wird. Viele Büros haben eine office kitty (kleine Kasse), aus der dann die Unkosten bezahlt werden. Wenn man neu ist, schadet es nie, nachzufragen, wer für die Unkosten aufgekommen ist und wie viel man schuldet: How much do I have to chip in?

Wenn Sie z. B. zu einer Weihnachtsfeier eingeladen sind kann es sein, dass einige Kollegen es vorziehen, als Nichtchristen nicht anwesend zu sein. Solch ein Fehlen wird nicht kommentiert, da es sich, vor allem in den USA, nicht schickt, nach der Religion der Arbeitskolleg/innen zu fragen. Sollten Sie jedoch von Ihren Kollegen persönlich über ihre Religion informiert worden sein, dann ist dies natürlich etwas ganz anderes. Eine Grußkarte mit Happy Holidays oder Season's Greetings oder Have a Happy Holiday and a Happy New Year ist dann immer willkommen.

Falsche Freunde

Man beschreibt häufig jemanden als sympathisch. Er ist ein ganz sympathischer Typ muss dabei mit He's a really nice guy oder He is a likeable guy übersetzt werden. Wenn man über seine Probleme spricht – was ja nicht sehr englisch ist, aber auch passieren kann - dann hofft man, das jemand zuhört, der mitfühlend bzw. verständnisvoll, also sympathetic reagiert. Sieht eine Person apart aus, dann ist dies mit striking oder distinctive zu übersetzen. Apart nämlich bedeutet, dass jemand abseits steht, beim Stehempfang beispielsweise: She is standing apart from the others.

Die moderne Bürowelt stellt jeden Einzelnen vor große Herausforderungen. Leute mit *vitaler* Energie und Durchsetzungskraft, people who are vigorous and energetic, sind daher immer gefragt. *Lebenswichtige* Entscheidungen stehen auf der Tagesordnung solcher Führungskräfte: Vital decisions are part of managers' daily agendas.

Wenn ein wichtiger *Brief* (letter) nicht pünktlich ankommt, kann es zu störenden Verzögerungen im Arbeitsablauf kommen. Klare *Instruktionen*, was in diesem Fall zu tun ist, wären nützlich: A clear brief on what to do as plan B would be helpful.

Jeder Chef freut sich, wenn sein ganzes *Personal* gut ausgebildet ist: All the personnel / staff is extremely well trained. Oft ist es eine schwierige *persönliche* Entscheidung, wen man noch in solch ein Team holen kann: It's difficult to decide personally who can join such a brilliant / marvelous team as yours.

Cultural and Other Activities / Kulturelle und andere Aktivitäten

Kulturelle Veranstaltungen sind für viele ein Muss in ihrer Freizeit. Beim Besuch von Theater, Konzert oder Ausstellung kann es jedoch peinlich werden, wenn man sich nicht zur Veranstaltung äußern kann. Wie Sie entspannt über Kunst und Kultur plaudern, zeigt Ihnen das folgende Kapitel.

Theater and Concerts / Theater und Konzerte

Theater and concert performances (Theatervorstellungen und Konzertbesuche), vor allem der Erfolg der ganz großen Künstler und ihr Leben im Rampenlicht, sind nicht nur ständiger Gesprächsstoff in den Medien, sondern auch ein beliebtes Montagmorgenthema im Büro. Tickets oder gift certificates (Geschenkgutscheine) zu diesen cultural events sind willkommene Geschenke für Geburtstage und andere Jubiläen, die Sie an der box office (Theaterkasse) erstehen können. Aber Achtung: Liebhaber dieser Kunstgattungen erfreuen sich häufig eines season tickets (Abonnements) und so sollten Sie vorsichtige Erkundigungen einziehen, damit die Überraschung mit den Konzert- oder Theaterkarten keine Enttäuschung nach sich zieht.

Im Konzert

Example

Mary is attending a concert at the Chicago Symphony. Part one of the program was Beethoven's Ninth, an all-time favorite. A standing ovation has already been given at intermission. Mary is so impressed by the performance that she starts talking to her neighbor.

Publikumsliebling
Pause

Mary: Oh, this is so wonderful. It's absolutely fabulous, isn't it?

wirklich fantastisch

Neighbor: You're right, it's fantastic. I have never heard such an accomplished performance of this symphony.

perfekte Aufführung

Mary: Indeed. Everything was just right; the tempi, the

In der Tat

precision and the reading of the music. — Deutung
Neighbor: Yes, I particularly enjoyed the vibrant choral sound and the eloquent interplay of choir and orchestra. What a magnificent piece of music! — gefiel vor allem; Wechselspiel

Useful phrases

Before the concert / Vor dem Konzert

- Sorry for letting you wait, but I had a hard time getting a cab! — es fiel mir schwer; (BE) taxi
- Excuse me, please. I think I have the seat next to you.
- Good evening. Today's program looks interesting, doesn't it? I've never heard music by an Estonian composer, have you? — das heutige Programm
- I don't think much of this conductor / director, do you? — halte wenig von; Dirigent
- I have season tickets. So far, I've enjoyed the series very much. — Vorstellungsreihe
- What a pity! The concert hall is only three quarters full. — Wie schade!

During intermission / Während der Pause

- Are you enjoying the concert?
- Will you join me in a drink? — Trinken Sie ein Glas mit mir?
- It's such a beautiful performance, isn't it? — Vorstellung, Aufführung
- Are you enjoying the concert?

- This is an unusually accomplished and attractive piece of music, don't you agree? — gelungen, perfekt
- The manuscript of this symphony must be quite sophisticated. — anspruchsvoll, kultiviert
- I really liked the Andante. It flowed so gracefully. — gefiel mir sehr gut

After the concert / Nach dem Konzert

- The music's originality and the orchestral effects were very well balanced. – I quite agree! — ganz meiner Meinung
- This was fabulous! What a performance. The acoustics in here are magnificent. — großartig
- I didn't know the encore they played, do you? — Zugabe
- See you the next time around. Bye now. — (AmE) hier
- I wouldn't mind a drink. — Ich hätte nichts gegen

At the Theater / Im Theater

Example

Mike has treated Martha to a theater performance. This was her surprise birthday present. — eingeladen; (BE) theatre

Martha: Mike, thank you so very much. I can't believe this. Here I am on my way to see the box office attraction of the season. They have been sold out for months. Did you know that? — ich bin dabei; Ist dir das klar?

Mike: Of course I did. To be honest, that doesn't — Natürlich

surprise me! After all, they've got nothing but raving reviews. Every newspaper and magazine I read was so unbelievably positive about their performance. — Schließlich; unglaublich zustimmend
Martha: Even the most highly acclaimed critic wrote a favorable criticism. And as you know, he typically picks on every little thing to complain about. — selbst; wie du ja weisst
Mike: That's right. By the way, do you want me to see you home afterwards? — nach Hause bringen
Martha: I'd appreciate that! — dafür wäre ich dir sehr dankbar

Useful phrases

Before the show / Vor der Aufführung

- It looks like today's performance is sold out. — sieht so aus als ob
- I beg your pardon. Is this row 15, aisle seat number 25? — Mittelgang
- May I please have a look at the program? I'd like to read up on today's performance. — Könnte, dürfte ich bitte
- This sure is an impressive building and a huge stage. — Das ist allerdings
- It would seem the auditorium seats 800 persons. — Wie es scheint

During intermission / Während der Pause

- Shall we go to the bar in the foyer and have something to drink? — Foyer
- This is terrific. I really like the actors.

- What an interesting piece. Its topic seems timeless. — Thema
- I like the mixture of a traditional stage setting and the avant-garde language use. — Bühnenbild

After the performance / Nach der Aufführung

- This is the best I have ever seen this play performed, it's above criticism. — über jede Kritik erhaben
- Bravo! I can see why they've got such great reviews. — Rezension, Kritik
- One can only have a favorable criticism of this performance. — wohlwollende Kritik
- The staging was most interesting. What do you think? — Inszenierung

Film and Literature / Film und Literature

Have you heard about this movie? Everybody is talking about it, let's go and see it! Kino ist universell, international, und selbst für ausgeprägte Kulturmuffel ein echtes Small Talk Thema: Egal ob über actors oder performers (Darsteller), den plot (Handlung), das script oder screenplay (Drehbuch) oder die sets and costumes (Ausstattung), das Kino bietet über Nationalitäten und Sprachbarrieren hinaus unendlich Stoff für Small Talk. Sobald man den Begriff Academy Award

Winning (mit dem Oscar ausgezeichnet) vernimmt, wartet jeder darauf, dass das Werk endlich im heimischen Kino gezeigt wird.

Example

Jim and Robin have won tickets to the first release of the new documentary. Though they both love movies very much, they have never been to a release. Jim's passion is historical films whereas Robin's favorite is romantic comedy.
Jim: Looking at the invitation, this is a formal event. Maybe you should wear a ball gown and I a tuxedo (Smoking).
Robin: Can you imagine!
Us among all these celebrities!
They had it on the news that all of the actors and actresses have confirmed their coming.
Jim: Yes, I heard that too. And the director will give a presentation right before they show the movie on how he researched every single detail of the film.
Robin: That must be so much work and effort.
Jim: I am sure it is. He is considered to be quite sophisticated in whatever he does.

Uraufführung
Ballkleid;
(BE) dinner jacket)
Stell Dir vor!
Berühmheiten
es kam in den Nachrichten; bestätigt
wird angesehen als

Useful phrases

Praising a film / Positive Filmkritik

- This film was directed by one of the most prestigious directors and it shows.
- This film was awarded best original score, accompaniment, best director and best cinematic photography.

renommiert
Partitur; Begleitmusik

- This movie is extraordinary; if you ask me, it's out of this world. — außergewöhnlich; wenn Sie mich fragen
- This glitzy appearance of the female protagonist is unlike her typical roles. — protzig; anders als

Movie jargon / Filmsprache

- Whoever stars under this director, will make a splash; that's common knowledge. — Furore machen; das ist bekannt
- Believe me, many actors are naturals. — Glauben Sie mir; Naturtalente
- The glamour of the modern movie world is so wonderful to see.
- Whenever a film has become a blockbuster, its music usually is also a big hit. — Knüller, ... in der Regel / meistens

Critical comments about the film / Kritische Kommentare zum Film

- I wasn't too fond of the short before the main movie. — nicht mögen; Kurzfilm
- If you ask me, the bit-part actors did in no way match the achievements of the other actors and actresses. — Wenn Sie mich fragen, ... Nebenrolle
- I thought that the pronounciation of all actors could have been better. — Aussprache
- I disliked the way the movie caricatured old music. — Ich mochte die Art nicht
- The film was way too long. It got really boring. — viel zu lang

Exhibits / Ausstellungen

Ihr Geschäftspartner ist Kunstliebhaber und lädt Sie zu einer Vernissage ein? Oder eine neue Kollegin möchte mit Ihnen eine exhibit (AmE) / exhibition (BE) (Ausstellung) besuchen? In Ausstellungen und im Museum können Sie auch guided tours (Führungen) machen. Neben paintings, drawings und sculpture, den Klassikern der Kunst, haben sich auch Installationen, Videos und mixed media in Museen und Sammlungen durchgesetzt.

Example

Many people are standing in line in the tourist information bureau in Washington, DC. It is a busy time of the year because ten different exhibits are being offered simultaneously. — Es ist viel los

Travel agent: Welcome to the city of exhibits. Would you like to know more about the special exhibit touring package? — Möchten Sie gerne

Tourist: Yes, I would. I only know about the exhibit on the old Italian masters. But please tell me more about the other exhibits. — Ja, gerne

Travel agent: I'd be happy to. The National Gallery of Arts has just opened two major exhibits: one is on Flemish tapestries and the other is on portraiture. Then, there is a special introduction to abstract art and cubism in the sculpture garden. — Das tue ich gern; flämische Gobelins; Porträtmalerei

Tourist: That sounds very interesting. Thank you very much for your help.

Useful phrases

Entering a museum / Beim Betreten eines Museums.

– Please be advised that eating and drinking are prohibited in all of the — Dürfen wir Sie darauf aufmerk-

museum exhibition halls.	sam machen
– Welcome to the gallery. Please note that all bags, coats and umbrellas must be checked in the checkroom.	Garderobe; (BE) auch Toilette
– Please bear in mind that picture taking is prohibited. A bit of advice: Leave your camera at home.	berücksichtigen Ein Rat
– It's sheer lunacy! Entry tickets for the temporary exhibit are already sold out for the next four weeks.	Das ist reiner Wahnsinn!

Touring an exhibit / Besuch einer Ausstellung

– There may be uncertainty as to who sketched these magnificent engravings.	es besteht Ungewissheit Radierungen
– Isn't it amazing how many masterpieces were donated by the endowment of the arts?	Ist es nicht erstaunlich Stiftung
– You can always reckon with a huge crowd in the room with still life paintings.	Sie können damit rechnen
– May I direct your attention to these large-format pictures.	Darf ich Ihre Aufmerksamkeit auf ... lenken
– The artist made her first strike with them.	Erfolg haben mit

Shopping at the museum store / Einkauf im Museumsshop

– Excuse me, do you sell reproductions of the Baroque age paintings?
– Do you happen to sell oversize postcards of the special exhibit? — Verkaufen Sie
– Do you also carry framed posters? — führen / im Sortiment haben
– How much is the catalog of the latest exhibit?

Shopping / Einkaufen

Neben Coca-Cola und Hamburger ist Shopping wohl eines der ersten englischen Wörter, das in die deutsche Sprache übernommen wurde. Doch Shopping kann viele Variationen und Bedeutungen haben. Für die meisten Amerikaner gehört Shopping zu einem der wichtigsten Freizeitvergnügen. Ein Nachmittag in der shopping mall kann bedeuten, dass man mit dem Vorsatz hingeht, lediglich window shopping, also einen Schaufensterbummel, zu machen – und dann mit bags of super deals und super sales (Schnäppchen) nach Hause kommt. Oder man wollte nur eben zu Walmart, stellt aber fest, dass im Kino nebenan der neueste Film gezeigt wird. Kein Wunder, dass man sich danach in einem ice-cream parlor (Eisdiele) einen ice-cream sundae (Eisbecher) gönnt.

Example

Kay and Robin are two high school students and have known each other since fourth grade. They often go to the mall together on a Sunday afternoon. Kay gives Robin a ring and leaves her a message on her answering machine in regard to their upcoming shopping adventure.

Kay: Hi Robin, how are you? Are we still on for our shopping tour on Sunday? I sure hope so because I need some new tennis shoes and a birthday present for Martha. I could pick you up at 2 o'clock. Please let me know.

grade – Klasse, (BE) form
gives a ring – anrufen
in regard to – bezüglich/wegen
Are we still on – geht das in Ordnung
pick you up – abholen

Useful phrases

Shopping for clothes / Kleidereinkaufen

- I'd like to try on a pair of jeans, relaxed fit, size 31. — lockerer Sitz
- Do you carry brand-name articles in men's fashion? — Markenartikel
- Could you please tell me whether there is a lingerie store nearby? — Unterwäsche
- Can I be of any help? – Yes, I am looking for a pair of children's shoes that are waterproof. — Kann ich irgendwie behilflich sein?

Grocery shopping / Lebensmittel einkaufen

- Excuse me, do you happen to sell certified organic foods? – Sure we do! — biologisch angebaut; Selbstverständlich
- How can I help you, madam? Have a look at the poultry. This is top quality — beste Qualität; zu

meat at a reasonable price. — vernünftigem Preis

– You will not believe this but these vegetables and fruits were home-grown in my grandfather's garden. — Sie werden es kaum glauben; selbst angebaut

Books and stationery / Bücher und Schreibwaren

– Do you by any chance have any glue / adhesive? — zufällig; Klebstoff

– I'd like to buy a ballpoint pen and 100 envelopes. — Kugelschreiber

– I'm afraid I bought the wrong ink cartridge. Can I exchange it, please?

– I think I could use some help. I'm looking for a novel about islands. Unfortunately, its title has slipped my mind. — Können Sie mir helfen?; ist mir entfallen

– Our selection of children's literature and short stories is downstairs. Mind your step, Sir! — Vorsicht Stufe!

At the drugstore (AmE) (chemist's (BE)) / In der Drogerie

– Baby food and diapers are to be found in aisle five. — Windeln, (BE) nappies

– Do you accept credit cards or checks? — Nehmen Sie Kreditkarten oder Schecks? (BE) cheque

– I am looking for a travel-size shampoo and setting lotion. — Ich suche nach; Festiger

– Do you carry hyper-allergenic soaps?	
– Could you please tell me when hair dye will be back in stock?	Haarfarbe nachliefern
– What are your business hours? – They are from 9 am to 5 pm.	Öffnungszeiten
– Last time, I bought dental floss on sale. Has this article been discontinued?	im Angebot ist ausgelaufen
– I have nothing but praise for the little general store at the corner. It carries the largest selection you can think of.	kann nur loben Tante Emma Laden größte Auswahl.
– To be honest, you'd better stay away from this store. It's outrageously expensive.	Ehrlich gesagt unerhört
– Why don't you try Compexpert? They're very reasonable in price if you're looking for computer supplies. I bet you'll like them; they're right up your alley.	Warum versuchen Sie nicht … ihre Wellenlänge
– I might be old-fashioned but I'm picky on good service when it comes to buying groceries.	pingelig; wenn es darum geht
– Excuse me, Sir, I desperately need (small) change for the parking meter; would you mind changing my bill?	(BE) (bank)note

Traveling / Unterwegs

Reisen, sei es aus geschäftlichen Gründen, also als business trip, zum purem Vergnügen oder in Form eines trip oder outing (kurzen Erholungsausflugs) sind heute selbstverständlich: Tours (kurze Rundreisen) laufen den journeys (langen Reisen) dabei den Rang ab. Auch wenn Sie unterwegs sind, ist es natürlich hilfreich, per Small Talk Kontakt mit seinen Mitreisenden aufzunehmen.

Traveling by train / Zugreisen

– He sure does a lot of traveling.	er ist häufig auf Reisen
– Could someone please assist me? I couldn't hear the announcement. Does the train to Vienna still leave from platform number 33?	Kann mir bitte jemand helfen? Wien
– I was struck speechless. Although the train left 30 minutes late, it made up time and arrived punctually.	Es verschlug mir die Sprache.
– She sure is a globe-trotter, to say nothing of her preference for exotic places.	Weltenbummler; ganz zu schweigen von
– You'll get the surprise of your life traveling by train through India.	Sie werden Ihr blaues Wunder erleben.
– You don't say! Don't you think the shuttle service to the downtown area should run more often than every hour on the hour?	Na, hören Sie mal zur vollen Stunde

Traveling by airplane / Flugreisen

- Let me tell you something! These package holiday charter flights are really a good deal. — Lassen Sie es sich gesagt sein; gutes Angebot.
- I stroke it lucky and got a standby ticket to Warsaw. — Ich hatte Glück; Warschau
- It strikes my fancy that smoking is no longer permitted in most airport terminals. — Es gefällt mir
- No sooner said than done. I called in for the phone lottery, won, and off I was to a one-week trip to the Canary Islands. — Gesagt, getan.
- It goes without saying that first class passengers are a little bit more pampered than economy class passengers. — Es ist selbstverständlich; verwöhnt

Traveling by bus / Busreisen

- Oh no! This doesn't help! The bus runs only twice a day. I'm afraid we are stuck here. — Das hilft uns nicht weiter; hängen bleiben
- This is unreal!
  The dining car is historic. In addition, the food they serve is out of this world. — Das ist unglaublich; absolut fantastisch
- There was a reaction time when the bus stopped abruptly. Thank God, nothing happened. — Schrecksekunde
- Whenever I take a trip on a bus with modern comfort, I have to think back to — Reisebus, (BE) coach

the times when coach meant a wagon pulled by horses.	Kutsche

Traveling by boat / Schiffsreisen

– Oh, I'm so excited. This is my first trip on a sailboat.	Ich bin so aufgeregt; (BE) sailing boat
– My dreams have come true! This Caribbean cruise is something else.	Wenn Träume wahr werden!
– The ferry is very popular and early reservations are highly recommended.	Fähre; sehr empfehlenswert
– In case you suffer from sea sickness, please use the sick bag in the seat pocket.	Falls ... Seekrankheit

Traveling by car / Im Auto unterwegs

– Traveling by car through New York City, you might get stuck in a traffic jam.	bleibt man womöglich im Stau stecken
– I often dash out of the office to beat rush-hour traffic.	sausen / stürmen / flitzen
– I can't wait to start working from home; I hate commuting day in and day out.	Ich kann's nicht erwarten;pendeln
– Just imagine: during rush hour, the fare for the metro is almost double the normal amount!	Stell dir vor

Kulturelle und sprachliche Tipps

Theater und Konzerte

Theater- und Konzertbesuche im Ausland folgen oft anderen Sitten. Für die Kleiderfrage gibt es keine leichte und eindeutige Antwort. Man trifft einerseits Konzertgänger, die den formal dress code mit tuxedo und ball gown oder evening dress befolgen, andererseits casual (leger) gekleidete in semiformal jeans kombiniert mit jacket. In Amerika ist es üblich, die Konzertsaison mit der Nationalhymne zu beginnen und sich dabei zu erheben. In der Regel herrschen in den USA auch strengere Rauchverbote als in Deutschland: Wenn Sie das Schild no smoking sehen, sollten Sie das Verbot unbedingt einhalten. Bei open-air Konzerten sind Getränke in bottles und cans oft verboten, es kann sein, dass nur Plastikbecher und –flaschen benutzt werden dürfen.

Kino, Museen und Ausstellungen

Bei Kinobesuchen in den USA werden meist auch keine alkoholischen Getränke, Bier inbegriffen, während der Vorstellung ausgeschenkt. Die Altersgrenze, mit der man in den USA in öffentlichen Lokalen alkoholische Getränke konsumieren darf, ist von Bundesland zu Bundesland verschieden und sollte unbedingt geachtet werden, denn jugendlich aussehende Besucher werden in Restaurants oder Bars gerne nach ihrem Ausweis gefragt.

Bei Besuchen von Museen und Ausstellungen sind Sicherheitsmassnahmen strenger als in Deutschland. Oft wird der

Alarm schon ausgelöst, wenn man sich zu nah an die Bilder beugt, um die kleine Beschriftung zu lesen. Fotografieren ist auch meist strengstens untersagt und kann Strafen zur Folge haben: Violators will be prosecuted.

Einkaufen und Höflichkeit

Beim Einkaufen in den USA wird der Preis der Waren, Lebensmittel ausgenommen, ohne steuerliche Gebühren angegeben. D.h. eine Jeans, die im Angebot mit 29.99 US Dollar ausgeschrieben ist, kann einiges mehr kosten, je nachdem, wie hoch die Steuersätze (local tax, state tax) des Bundeslandes auf clothes sind. In Großbritannien wird die Mehrwertsteuer mit VAT, sprich value added tax angegeben.

Bei Reisen mit der Bahn, dem Flugzeug oder dem Bus fallen diejenigen unangenehm auf, die nicht geduldig Schlange stehen (queuing, standing in line) und höflich abwarten, bis sie an der Reihe sind. Es gehört zum guten Ton, sich sofort zu entschuldigen – I'm awfully sorry! Excuse me! Oh, I'm so sorry! – sollte man jemanden aus Versehen im Gedränge anrempeln (bump into someone).

Falsche Freunde

Bei Kunstgesprächen sollte man das deutsche Wort Art nicht mit dem englischen art zu verwechseln: I've always been a fan of ancient art (Ich war schon immer ein Liebhaber antiker Kunst), aber: She's the kind of person who can listen carefully (Sie gehört zu der Art von Menschen, die genau zuhören können).

Erfolgreiche Spots für Film und Fernsehen sind Kurz- oder Werbefilme (commercials / ads). Doch sagt Ihnen jemand we meet at the same spot, dann meint er nicht das Kino, sondern dieselbe Stelle wie beim letzten Treffen. On the spot hingegen bedeutet sofort.

Beim Einkaufen kann die Vermischung vom Englischen und Deutschen zu den interessantesten Verwechslungen führen. Im Kleidergeschäft gibt es jeans und pants (trousers BE) in der Hosenabteilung. Einen hose, nämlich den Schlauch, werden Sie nur in der Gartenabteilung finden.

Beim Kauf von Unterwäsche ist Vorsicht geboten: Bei der Dame ist der slip der Unterrock, der Slip hingegen ein Pluralwort: panties. Bei den Herren fragen Sie den amerikanischen Verkäufer bitte nach underpants oder (a pair of) briefs, den Briten nach pants. Hat Sie dieser Einkauf recht angestrengt, dann suchen Sie doch bitte einen Stuhl (chair) oder erholen Sie sich im nächsten Stehcafe auf einem Hokker (stool) bei einer guten Tasse Kaffee. Die Milch wird Ihnen dort hoffentlich nicht in der Tüte (carton), sondern in einem Kännchen serviert. Haben Sie Ihre Mitbringsel (memento, souvenir) auch schön in Kartons (cardboard boxes) verpakken lassen?

Favorite Small Talk Topics / Klassische Small Talk Themen

Die Klassiker beim Small Talk sind Themen, die uns persönlich angehen: das Wetter, Hobbys, Kinder und Familie, Haustiere, der Garten. Zum Bereich Hobby gehören natürlich auch Sport und das Thema Autos – nicht nur für Männer.

The Weather / Das Wetter

Kaum ein Thema des Small Talk hat eine solch ausgeprägte Tradition wie das Thema Wetter: Für alle fühlbar, für keinen übersehbar, Auslöser für Kopfschmerzen oder wahre Energieschübe, entscheidend für die Freizeitgestaltung ist es ein ergiebiges topic, um mit Menschen in Kontakt zu kommen: Die Bemerkung It's a lovely day today, isn't it? lädt dazu ein, den schönen Tag auf verschiedenste Weisen zu loben: Bejahend mit einem Yes, indeed! oder enthusiastisch: Oh, yes, it's such a beautiful morning. Vielleicht hat ein It would be the perfect day for a game of golf or a tennis match sogar eine Verabredung zum Sport zur Folge.

Gerade die Briten werden gerne wegen ihrer ausgeprägten meteorological observations und ihrem engen Bezug zum Wetter mit Small Talk Fragen nach der weather situation (Wetterlage), dem weather report / forecast (Wetterbericht) oder dem weather outlook for tomorrow / till Tuesday (Wetteraussichten für morgen / bis Dienstag), um ein kurzes meteorologisches Statement gebeten. Sie werden Ihnen gerne über eventuelle change in weather (Wetterwechsel), über sudden drops in temperature (Wetterstürze), zu erwartenden storm warnings (Regen und Sturmwarnungen) Auskunft geben.

Example

It's early in the morning. Julie opens the front door of the house to pick up the newspaper when she sees her neighbor just stepping out of the house, too.
Julie: Good morning, Kay. It's a beautiful day today,

isn't it?
Kay: Oh, hi, Julie. Yes, it is a lovely day today, indeed. The kids will love it. Today's their last baseball game of the season.
Julie: You don't say! The last three games were hit by thunderstorms. I still shiver thinking about how cold I felt.
Kay: Yes, I remember, that must have been the ugliest day of the season.
Julie: Maybe today we'll need some suntan lotion and headgear. Look how bright the sun is already!
Kay: Yes, I love it this way. And don't forget your sunglasses.
Julie: Enjoy this beautiful day. See you later.

Nicht möglich! von Gewittern heimgesucht das war wohl vielleicht, (BE) perhaps; Kopfbedeckung Bis dann

Useful phrases

General weather descriptions / Allgemeine Wetterbeschreibungen

- Whenever I hear raindrops falling on my window, I remember my time in Asia and the ups and downs of the monsoon season. — Jedesmal wenn / so oft; das Auf und Ab
- In summer the humidity here is unbearable. — Luftfeuchtigkeit
- I was far from believing that this northern region has such mild winters and dry summers. — Ich war weit davon entfernt, zu glauben
- So what you are saying is that you had a record-breaking winter with freezing temperatures way below the normal range. — Was du sagen willst; weit

Weather forecasts / Wettervorhersagen

– Based on my experience it is going to be another gorgeous Indian summer day.	Meiner Erfahrung nach Spätsommer
– According to the weather forecast I heard on the radio, we can expect a foggy morning but dazzling sunshine in the afternoon.	Laut Wettervorhersage blendend, grell
– Most of the day will be overcast with temperatures in the low 60s.	bewölkt Fahrenheit, etwa 20°C
– There is a storm warning until tomorrow night; most likely it's going to start drizzling right away.	wahrscheinlich fängt es gleich an zu tröpfeln.

Describing bad weather / Schlechtes Wetter beschreiben

– Dreadful weather, isn't it? – You can say that again.	schaurig / furchtbar
– The weather's been awful lately, hasn't it?	
– I'm afraid that another heavy overnight snowfall will bring nothing but chaos.	Ich befürchte

– She refused to believe that they had closed the roads because of the dangerous conditions.	Sie wollte es einfach nicht glauben
– Don't worry! I 'm going to be really careful driving home on slippery roads.	Mach Dir keine Sorgen; glatte Fahrbahnen

Weather idioms / Redewendungen rund um das Wetter

– I'm sorry, I can't join you. I'm under the weather.	sich nicht wohl fühlen
– Sorry, I haven't the foggiest idea.	nicht die leiseste Ahnung haben
– She's been on cloud nine ever since she first met him.	im 7. Himmel
– They were all off like (greased) lightning.	blitzschnell

Traveling, Cities and Countries / Reisen, Städte und Länder

Have a safe journey! oder Enjoy your trip! sind die gängigsten Abschiedsformeln für alle diejenigen, die abfahrbereit in den Urlaub sind. Die Mobilität und Reiselust unserer Zeit hat neue Dimensionen erreicht. Booking a trip (eine Reise buchen) – das tut man im Internet. Die Auswahl an Pauschalreisen reicht von Kultur- und Bildungsreisen über Erholungsurlaube, Strandurlaube bis hin zu adventure trips (Abenteuerreisen) und Sportferien. Ein trip ist generell kürzer als eine journey, bei voyage handelt es sich um eine Schiffsreise, die mit dem Wort cruise noch als Kreuzfahrt spezifiziert werden kann.

Die wichtigste Voraussetzung zum Reisen jedoch sind ein paar freie Tage – ein wichtiger Gesprächsstoff, nicht nur im Büro: I got three days off (ich habe drei Tage frei bekommen), Friday's my day off. Geraten Sie bei Schilderungen des Wochenendes nicht durcheinander: Wenn Sie übers Wochenende bei Ihrer Familie sind, heißt es I'll visit my family over the weekend, fahren Sie jedoch weg, muss es I'll be going away for the weekend heißen. Nutzen Sie Ihren Urlaubsanspruch vacation privilege (BE holiday entitlement), denn Erholung, nämlich recovery oder recuperation sowie rest, relaxation (Entspannung) bieten neben der recreation (Freizeitgestaltung) äußerst beliebten Gesprächsstoff.

Reisen sind für den Small Talk ein unerschöpfliches Thema. Fragen wie How was your trip to Michigan? oder Where are you off to oder How was your tour of Florida? beantwortet der vacationer (BE holidaymaker) gerne. Die Vorfreude auf den kommenden Wochenendtrip ist immer ein dankbares Small Talk Thema: I can't wait for the weekend; we're going on a mountain hike in Vermont. Thank God, it's Friday: Time for a little outing at the Great Lakes.

Example

Francis and Laura have both just returned from their vacation. They meet in a café in order to talk about their experiences.	
Francis: So, you went to the US. Thank you for sending me a postcard.	Vielen Dank für die Karte
That's very kind of you. I can't wait to hear more about your trip.	Ich muss unbedingt
Laura: The trip was absolutely wonderful. I had the best time of my life. We had booked a package tour that included flight, mobile home and entry tickets to the national parks.	völlig
Francis: That sounds really exciting. I bet you covered a lot of miles.	sehr viel herumgekommen
Laura: Absolutely, you have no idea how huge that country is. The open space is beyond description. It's truly overwhelming.	Ganz recht! Du kannst dir nicht vorstellen wie; wirklich
Francis: What part of the country did you like best?	
Laura: That's hard to say, but I'd say the southwest.	schwer zu sagen

Useful phrases

Going on vacation (BE holiday)/ Ferien machen

– Linda is on a trip to Topeka, it's her day off today.	ihr freier Tag
– When are you going on holiday?	Wann habt ihr Ferien?

- When is your vacation? — (AmE) Ferien
- We're going to Lake Michigan for a rest / to relax. — zur Erholung
- Have a good rest! — gute Erholung!
- William and Annie are planning to go on holiday together with destination New York! — Ferien machen; Reiseziel

Praising travel comments / Lobende Reisekommentare

- How was your trip? – It was the best ever. — der aller, allerbeste
- Did you have a nice vacation? – Yes, I had a wonderful time. Everything was just right. — genau richtig
- Our cruise was a once-in-a-life-time experience. I can only recommend it. — Kreuzfahrt; empfehlen
- People in the countryside were extraordinarily warm and hospitable. I never would have thought so. — gastfreundlich; Hätte ich nie gedacht.

Negative travel comments / Negative Reisekommentare

- I'm afraid our accommodations were not what we expected. — Unterkunft
- The organization of our trip did not meet our standards. — entsprach unseren Anforderungen nicht

– There was more than one problem with our tourist guide. In my opinion, he was poorly prepared. — Meines Erachtens / meiner Meinung nach

– Unfortunately, our vacation was basically rained out. — Leider; verregnet

Geographic descriptions / Geographische Landschaftsbeschreibung

– The rest area in the rolling hills was wonderful. One had a panoramic view of the whole valley. — Rastplatz; Hügellandschaft

– I don't know how they do it but the beaches were immaculate: no litter, no cigar butts, absolutely nothing. — Unglaublich!

– What are your plans for the Easter break? — Was planen Sie

– We're still uncertain as to whether to take the children along or to vacation alone. — unsicher ob, ungewiß ob

– How was your vacation? I'd like to hear all about it.

– As far as I know, the terrain is mostly rugged and not good for biking. — So weit ich weiß; zerklüftet

– Did you know that the islands are famous for their mountainous and volcanic origin? — berühmt für; bergig

– Let me tell you something: the less well-known part of the island is very beautiful, especially all the way down at the lighthouse. It's worth the trouble.	der Mühe wert sein
– Take my word for it: three days of beach volleyball energize you for the next three months. I promise!	Glaub mir; versprochen
– During a girl talk I told my colleague that she should learn to relax a bit more and take it easy.	Frauengespräch
– How about going along the fertile valleys and enjoying the rich vegetation?	Wie wär's, wenn

Special names / Besondere Namen

– I quite believe it! Southern France and South Africa are favorite tourist destinations.	Das glaube ich gern!
– Just imagine! You're on your dream vacation in Venice and Vienna and your package tour includes four concerts.	Denken Sie nur!; Venedig
– Whenever I think of Aix-la-Chapelle and Munich, I have fond memories of the famous chocolate and Bavarian sausages.	Aachen; München; liebe Erinnerungen
– I wonder whether we could reach an agreement and for our next vacation travel to the Baltic Sea.	Ich frage mich ....; sich einigen; Ostsee

- They say you went on your first high mountain climbing tour. How interesting! — Man erzählt sich
- Last year my mother went to see the famous Christmas bazaar in Nuremberg. She satisfied a lifelong wish. — (sich) erfüllen / befriedigen
- May I warn you about Bejing's very hectic life style? — Ich warne Sie vor Peking

Describing cities / Städtebeschreibungen

- I was absolutely speechless the first time I saw pointed gables over 500 years old. — vollkommen sprachlos ... spitze Giebel
- You may thank your stars that your old historic town has never been destroyed. — Du kannst von Glück sagen
- It's a matter of opinion whether the picturesque riverside or the lovingly renovated city hall is the town's picture postcard view number one. — Es ist Ansichtssache malerisches Flußufer Rathaus
- It's hard to believe that the half-timbered houses of the 15th century are still not on the national register. — Kaum glaublich ... Fachwerk ... Denkmalschutz
- The city council should awaken awareness of the historic sites of the Middle Ages. — öffentliches Interesse wecken ... Mittelalter

Description of countries / Länderbeschreibung

- Brazil's famous tropical rain forest is spoiled by cattle farmers. – Don't let that concern you. — Mach Dir deswegen keine Sorgen.
- South America with its gigantic mountain range and rich vegetation is considered one of the natural wonders of the world. — gilt als; Naturwunder
- After my visit to the former Eastern bloc countries I had to revise my opinion: people are very open, hospitable, and most eager to meet foreigners. - I should think so! — umdenken; Das will ich meinen!
- May I remind you that India's diversity in cultures is beyond belief. — Darf ich Sie daran erinnern

Tourist information about countries / Touristeninformation über Länder

- I'm at a loss about what to do. Shall I go on a package tour with cultural highlights or hang out on the beach? — Ich weiß nicht, was ich tun soll. ... herumlungern ...
- I know for certain: this is the best ski resort you can think of. There is year-round skiing and the peaks average an altitude of 3,000 meters. — Ich weiß bestimmt; Gipfel

- That's not how I'd visualized my vacation. Instead of kayaking, I spent two weeks in the hospital due to food poisoning. — So hatte ich mir das nicht vorgestellt
- If you ever travel to the British Isles, you should never push to the front of a line. The British are fond of social etiquette and queuing. — vordrängen; anstellen

Instructions how to get someplace / Wegbeschreibungen

- In order to avoid a tour through the jammed downtown area, follow the signs for loop number 495. — verstopft; Umgehungsstraße
- Follow the main road until you come to a traffic light. Make a left and continue until you come to a traffic circle. There you take the second exit. — Links abbiegen; Kreisverkehr; (BE) roundabout
- The city hall / town hall is right next to the market place. You can't miss it. It is richly decorated. — Rathaus; verpassen / versäumen
- The bank is only two doors down from the post office. Just follow the street with cobblestones. — Kopfsteinpflaster

Hobbies and Leisure Activities / Hobbys und Freizeitgestaltung

Canyoning, Bungee Jumping, Sky Diving, Rafting – die Begriffe für ungewöhnliche Sportarten werden meist direkt aus dem Englischen ins Deutsche übernommen, das gilt auch für den Breitensport wie Snowboarden oder Roller Skaten. Je intensiver der Arbeitstag vor dem Computer, desto größer die Abenteuerlust und der Spass an Sport und Fitness in der Freizeit. Wo man nur hinschaut, schießen fitness centers, spas und wellness centers aus dem Boden. Doch auch cultural events (kulturelle Veranstaltungen) oder arts and crafts (Basteln) erfreuen sich großer Beliebtheit. Nicht zu vergessen sind auch die unzähligen Musikvereine oder Klubs, die für das soziale Wohl ihrer Mitglieder sorgen.

Example

John has moved to a new town which is much smaller than the one he used to live in. In order to learn more about the clubs and social life of the town, he visits the tourist information bureau. — wo er wohnte

John: Hello. Do you happen to have information about the different clubs and leisure activities in the area? I'm new in town. I just moved here from San Francisco. — haben Sie vielleicht

Agent: Welcome to Little Creek then! I hope you'll like it here. Do you have any special interests? — Haben Sie besondere Interessen?

John: Actually, I do. I like to sing and play cards and board games. But in summer, I prefer being outside. — Brettspiele

Agent: Well, then I think you've come to the right place. — sie sind genau richtig hier

Let me give you a brief overview of what is offered. — Überblick

John: Please do. That sounds like a good idea. — Bitte tun Sie das

Agent: There are two choirs in town. The one called chorus, performs mostly sacred music, be it the classics, gospels or oratories. The other one prefers folk music and musicals. Every first Saturday of the month, the local pub has its "play day" for board games and cards. Bingo and canasta are very popular around here. With respect to outdoor activities, there are two new ones. First, there's local history. That might include a guided tour of the local museum, an archaeological excavation, or guided nature walks. The next one is on local birds and their habitat. You might take a look at these brochures and let me know if I can be of further help.

Chöre
geistliche Musik
in Bezug auf
Ausgrabung
Broschüren
ob ich weiter behilflich sein kann

John: Thank you very much for your great assistance. I'm sure I'll find something to do. Bye now.

Unterstützung

Useful phrases

Games / Spiele

– For all I know he's a real poker face; you'd better not bet when playing cards with him.

Soviel ich weiß

– My last vacation was a nightmare. It rained day in, day out and we could do nothing but play checkers or chess.

Albtraum
Damespiel (BE draughts) oder Schach

– Don't be a poor sport! Shuffle the cards well and have your right-hand neighbor cut them. You'd better play by the rules.

Sei kein Spielverderber; Mischen; abheben

- That's life, if you have a bad hand. — So ist nun mal das Leben; ein schlechtes Blatt

Board games /Brettspiele

- Pachisi (Parcheesi, parchesi, parchisi) certainly is a game for young and old. — Mensch ärgere dich nicht
- That beats me! I don't have the brains for strategic thinking in chess, I'd rather play backgammon. — Das ist mir zu hoch! ich spiele lieber
- That's the limit! You won five chess games in a row. Enough is enough. — Das ist die Höhe!
- You're a spoil sport! Checkers / draughts can be so much fun if people don't cheat. — Spielverderber; Dame
- It's about as broad as it's long whether I have white or black; I always win my chess games. — Das ist gehupft wie gesprungen.

Music activities as hobbies / Musik und Freizeit

- I've always dreamt of playing the piano or grand piano. — Klavier; Flügel
- I really want you to think your choice of music instruments through. It's a burden to carry a harp around. — gründlich über etwas nachdenken
- I knew it from the very beginning. The violin soloist is a new boy wonder. — Wunderknabe

- I'm impressed with our new conductor. — beeindruckt; Dirigent
- Looking back to my high school time, I've got very fond memories of being a member of the marching band. — blicke ich zurück auf; Blaskapelle
- Because of my work, I unfortunately can only attend rehearsals biweekly. — Proben; alle 14 Tage

Different interests / Verschiedene Interessen

- If you like to read a lot, you might want to join a literary club / society. — wollen Sie vielleicht
- Whenever the subject of coins comes up, my Grandma talks her head off. — das Thema; reden wie ein Buch
- Don't you like to socialize from time to time, to go to discos, bars and open air music events? — gesellig sein
- The senior citizen's club offers an incredible range of health programs. You wouldn't want to take a closer look at it, would you? — unglaubliches Angebot; Wollen Sie (es) sich nicht
- Not having exercised for over a week, I feel nothing but stiffness. To say the least, I'm not in shape. — Gelinde gesagt, um es milde auszudrücken ...; nicht fit sein
- I can only agree with the experts that swimming is one of the healthiest types of sport. — Ich kann nur zustimmen

– Reaching the peak at sunset is a mind-boggling moment, every time anew.	umwerfend/überwältigend
– Hawaii is the perfect surfing place. Everybody is bragging about it.	prahlen
– On my last skiing adventure I came across the most beautiful piste. It was hidden way up in the valley, just the slope for you.	etwas zufällig finden; Hang, Abhang
– Playing a tennis match is not as simple as that. It takes a lot of practice and patience.	ist gar nicht so einfach
– I'm not too fond of overcrowded ski slopes because they are quite dangerous.	nicht so gern haben, mögen
– Running a marathon is absolutely not my cup of tea.	nicht von Interesse sein
– You can't make me believe that skating isn't dangerous. It poses way too many health risks for people with weak ankles.	mir einreden; aufwerfen
– May I tell you that jogging in the midday heat is very dangerous: it puts a strain on your circulation.	Darf ich Ihnen sagen, dass; belasten / strapazieren

Children, Gardening and Pets / Kinder, Gartenarbeit und Haustiere

Small talk über persönliche Interessen wie Gartenarbeit und Gartenpflege oder Haustiere und ihre artgerechte Haltung garantiert oft sehr angenehme Unterhaltungen. Es scheint einem generell leichter zu fallen, sich über Dinge zu äußern, die man gerne macht oder hat.

Viele englische Small Talker kommen daher gerne ohne Umschweife auf ihre Kinder oder ihre Enkelkinder zu sprechen. Viele grannies (Großmütter) und grandpas (Großväter) haben Fotos ihrer Enkel in der Brieftasche und zeigen sie schnell und gerne vor: This is my youngest grandchild. She just turned two. Isn't she adorable? Oder My oldest granddaughter just married. Her husband is a real sweetie (ein wahrer Schatz), too. Vergleiche mit der Familie des Gegenüber und ihrer Genealogie sind die unvermeidliche Folge: We're considered a large family, but in comparison to yours we're just a small bunch of Irish immigrants.

Example

It's parents' evening at the local elementary school. Some of the parents take the opportunity to talk about their children on a more personal level.	nehmen die Gelegenheit wahr ... auf persönlicherer Ebene
Carol: Hi Alice, how are things with Bob?	wie geht es eigentlich
Alice: Hi, Carol. Bob is doing so-so. He sprained his ankle and might not be able to play in the upcoming tennis tournament.	geht es so la-la Fuß verstaucht bevorstehenden

Carol: Oh dear, that doesn't sound too good, does it? Tell him I wish him all the best. — das klingt nicht gut
Alice: How is Celia? Didn't she try out for the theater group? — sich bewerben
Carol: Yes, she did, and guess what: she made it. — rate mal
Alice: Congratulations!
Carol: Thank you. She's all into it. Can you imagine my daughter reading and enjoying literature? Miracles happen! — mit Leib und Seele dabei

Useful phrases

Family / Familie

- My family immigrated at the beginning of the 20th century. My grandmother comes from Norway; my father is half Italian and half Polish.
- If I'm not mistaken, my cousin did her internship in your company last summer. — Wenn mich nicht alles täuscht
- One part of my family emigrated from Germany to Israel; the other lives in the greater New York City area. — in und rund um New York
- My family is very close. Each year we all meet at my uncle's for Thanksgiving. — Meine Familie hängt sehr aneinander
- As is customary, I don't get along that well with my parents-in-law, but we make the best of it. — Wie das so üblich ist; wir arrangieren uns

– In reality, I moved to the south to please my husband because his brothers and sisters live there with their children. — Eigentlich; meinem Mann zuliebe
– Because we don't have children of our own we take all the more interest in our niece. My wife is her godmother. — desto mehr Anteil nehmen wir; Patentante
– I'm twice divorced. Let me introduce you to my third wife, Agnes. — Ich bin bereits zweimal geschieden

Talking about children's school performance / Über die Leistungen von Kindern sprechen

– My son just graduated from high school. — (AmE) absolviert
– My daughter is doing really well at school. She is on the honors roll and therefore plans to go to college. — Ehrung für besondere akademische Leistung
– My nephew loves doing math and science experiments. He's so unlike the rest of the family, you wouldn't believe it. — verschieden / anders als / unähnlich
– My niece has a natural talent for learning languages. I wonder whether she got that from her mother. — Ob sie das von ihrer Mutter geerbt hat.

Children and sports / Kinder und Sport

- My niece is exceptionally / extremely athletic. She plays on the school's volleyball varsity team. — außergewöhnlich; Schulmannschaft
- My son loves all ball games but dislikes gymnastics and any type of endurance sports. — Ausdauersportarten
- All of my children are fanatic and assiduous about aquatic sport, regardless of whether it is swimming, diving or high diving. — ausdauernd; egal ob; Turmspringen
- We are a typical American family: My son is the captain of the football team and my daughter is a cheerleader. — eine typisch amerikanische Familie

Children and their pets / Kinder und ihre Haustiere

- My youngest daughter Helen is longing for a guinea-pig. Do you know anything about keeping those pets? — Meerschweinchen; wissen Sie, wie
- My half-brother Bill performs equestrian acrobatics. As a child he had no interest whatsoever in sports or horses. — nicht das leiseste Interesse;
- My granddaughter Vera is allergic to cats and dogs. That's why my daughter bought her a tortoise called Pucki. — Daher; Landschildkröte

– Did you know that our trainee has her own little zoo: one rabbit, two white mice and a parakeet / budgerigar (budgie)? — Wissen Sie eigentlich ... Praktikant; Wellensittich

Describing children / Kinder schildern

– My oldest grandchild looks just like her father, but her personality is just like her mother's. — vom Charakter her, kommt sie ganz nach ihrer Mutter
– My nephew is so cute, you have no idea. — unvorstellbar
– My elder daughter inherited my husband's passion for music. — erbte
– My stepchild was very shy at first but has now opened up. — zugänglich werden

Gardening /Gartenarbeit

Gardening (Gartenarbeit) erfreut und entspannt die Menschen wohl überall auf dem Globus, selbst wenn sie nur ein winziges Fleckchen Grün oder lediglich einen Balkon haben. Den Engländern und Japanern wird eine wahre gardening obsession (Gartenmanie) nachgesagt. Jeder passionierte Gärtner entwickelt seine eigenen secret home remedies (Geheimrezepte), um die schönsten Früchte zu ernten und das beste Gemüse oder die elegantesten Blumen zu ziehen. Über pruning (Baumschnitt) und cultivating / growing (Pflanzenzucht), über vermin control (Ungezieferbekämpfung), lawnmower und sprinkler können passionierte Gärtner von Hecke zu Hecke stundenlang philosophieren – der Garten und die Gartenarbeit sind eine wahre Fundgrube für unverkrampften Small Talk.

Example

Neighbors Lesley and Ted are both working in their garden.

Lesley: Hi, Ted. Here we go again, there's always something to do, isn't there? — *es geht wieder los*

Ted: There sure is. I'm glad it rained so it's easier to weed out.

If there is one thing I hate, it's a garden running to weeds. — *wenn ich etwas hasse; verunkrauten*

Lesley: Ted, let me tell you. As much as you tender your garden, weeds don't even have a chance! How are your cucumbers this year? Mine look a little bit on the small side. — *pflegen; eher klein*

Ted: That's right, but they taste delicious. The tomatoes look pretty good, too. My grandchild Fay called already to see when she can come and pick Grandpa's tomatoes.

Lesley: Is that so? Make sure to let her know she's always welcome to help me pick berries and cut the lawn. — *Stimmt das?*

Ted: Will do. I'd better go in and help prepare dinner. Bye. — *Wird gemacht.*

Lesley: Bye now.

Useful phrases

– Look at your garden! Everything grows so nicely. You have a green thumb, just like your mother.

– I've had it! I've tried everything this year, but my tomatoes are not doing well at all. — Mir langt's! / Ich verliere die Geduld

– Let's play it by ear when I come and cut your lawn. A storm's brewing. — ohne Planung / spontan

– I just don't know when to tender my garden. The weather has been so bad, it's not fit to turn a dog out. — Bei diesem Wetter jagt man keinen Hund vor die Tür.

– If you talk to your plants, they'll grow better. – To each his / her own. — Jedem das Seine.

– This year my pumpkins are really not doing well. I have no clue what's happening. — keine Ahnung haben

– If the drought continues, this may have serious consequences for my garden. — Trockenheit ... kann ernste Folgen haben

– Be that as it may, I assure you that I can taste the difference between home-grown tomatoes and the ones from the store. — Das mag sein, wie es will; versichern, zusichern

– I dare say that my neighbor's herbal garden needs major work to be done. — Allerdings; Kräutergarten

– So far so good. My potatoes were not hit by the Colorado beetle. — So weit, so gut; Kartoffelkäfer

– Rose-bushes are supposed to be cut in autumn, but experience has taught me they'll blossom better after a springtime cut. — sollte man schneiden; (AmE) fall Herbst

- No home gardener likes snails among the lettuce plants, neither do I. — Schnecken; ich auch nicht
- My neighbor always shows off with his really fancy rakes. I still use Grandpa's and that does the job. — angeben; das tut es auch
- Not every gardener believes in adding dung / manure to his vegetables. — Dünger

Pets / Haustiere

Wie viele Haustiere auf der ganzen Welt gehalten werden, wird man wohl nicht genau beziffern können. Doch muss es sich um Millionen von Tieren handeln. Diese kleinen Freunde sind ein beliebtes Small Talk Thema; gerade Hundebesitzer schließen über ihren collie, German shepherd, poodle oder dachshund schnell Kontakte.

Example

Mr Miller walks his dog Max, a dalmatian, every day at 5 o'clock in the morning. They usually meet Mrs. Smith with her Irish setter in the park and have a chat. — Hund ausführen; Dalmatiner

Mr Miller: How are you today? You are not going to believe this but I had to call the veterinarian emergency last night. My dog was playing with his ball when he started to choke and whine.

Mrs Smith: Oh no! That sounds terrible. What had happened? — würgen ... jammern

Mr Miller: Well. There was a little pebble stuck to the ball and my dog must have bitten on that. Everything is fine now, thank God. — Alles ist wieder gut

Useful phrases

– Oh dear! My new neighbor is a dog-fancier. He's got five dogs and three puppies.	Ach je; Hundeliebhaber; Welpen
– I really like the new kennel. They take very good care of the animals.	gern mögen Hundeheim
– Did you see the ad? They just came out with a new bird seed.	auf den Markt bringen; Vogelfutter
– My family has to talk over what new pet to get: a tortoise or a rabbit.	besprechen; Kanichen
– It couldn't have been better! When we took our grandchildren to the zoo, the chickens were just hatching.	Es hätte besser nicht sein können ausschlüpfen

Sports and Cars / Sport und Autos

Sport und Autos sind schon lange keine Männerdomäne mehr: In den USA sind die cheerleaders längst nicht mehr die einzigen Frauen im Baseball- oder Basketballstadium. Frauenteams gewinnen die renommierte Rallye Paris-Dakar und im Breitensport Golf treten Frauen ebenso bei Wettkämpfen an, wie sie es schon seit Jahren im Tennis oder im Reitsport tun.

Neben Politik und Wirtschaft werden wenig Themen so international diskutiert wie der Sport: Man stößt dabei auf hohe Identifikationsbereitschaft und das ist immer eine gute Voraussetzung für Small Talk. Dank weltweiter Fernsehübertragungen von internationalen Wettkämpfen wie den Autorennen in Monza oder Monte-Carlo, den world championships (Weltmeisterschaften) in den diversen Sportgattungen oder den Olympic Games / The Olympics (Olympischen Spielen) gibt es endlosen Gesprächsstoff.

In den USA werden insbesondere baseball und football – nicht zu verwechseln mit unserem Fussball, der im Amerikanischen Englisch soccer heißt, diskutiert. Die NBA National Basketball-Liga und der Superbowl sind abendfüllende Small Talk Themen. In Großbritannien erfüllen das Golfen und das Polo-Spiel eine ähnlich kommunikative Funktion.

Example

Larry and Peter are both very much into sports. They watch every soccer and basketball game on TV. In addition, they are both great tennis players and keep their bodies in shape.	sehr begeistert von; zusätzlich
Larry: Hi Peter, this is Larry calling. Did you watch the basketball game? It was a close game and quite nerve wracking, up to the very last minute.	knapp ausgegangen; Nerven aufreibend
Are we still on to do our family day at the stadium?	Geht das in Ordnung mit
Peter: It's fine with us. We could first watch the game, then have a picnic in the park and play baseball and basketball with our children.	Geht klar.
Peter: That sounds like a marvellous idea. By the way, my youngest daughter just made the softball little league. In her first game she even hit her first homerun. She is so excited, you can't imagine.	Übrigens; unvorstellbar
Larry: That's terrific. I've told you before that she has a feel for the ball. I guess she wouldn't mind playing with the boys, would she?	toll/fantastisch; ich schätze / glaube
Peter: Not at all. She's a tough kid and very competitive.	kämpferisch / wettbewerbsfreudig

Useful phrases

Type of sports / Sportarten

– Swim events, be it breaststroke or butterfly, are fun to watch on TV. Why don't you join me to watch the championships?	Brustschwimmen; Delfin

– To be honest, I could live without formula one races, but they are a nine days' wonder, wherever one goes. — Ehrlich gesagt; Tagesgespräch

– I can only hope that you find a good tennis coach for your son. He's very talented and should make the most of it. — das Beste daraus machen

– Mike is usually a sport, but when he plays rugby, he turns into a beast. — netter Kerl sein

Sports equipment / Sportausrüstung

– Good tennis rackets are still quite expensive, so I tend to borrow mine, since I don't play very often. — Tennisschläger

– I'm at a loss as to where to buy boxing gloves. Boxing equipment is still scarce. — Ich weiß nicht aus noch ein; selten

– It takes a skilled hand to use a hockey stick and lots of practice to score many goals. — Man braucht geschickte Hände

– If you play golf in Germany, you are usually considered to be well-off. In other countries golf is a sport for the masses. — wohlhabend; Breitensport

Idioms with sports language / Redewendungen aus dem Sport

– We have to level the playing field (football). — Gleiche Voraussetzungen für alle.

- That's par for the course (golf). — Das ist ganz normal.
- The ball's in your court (tennis). — Du bist am Zug.
- It's back to square one (board games). — Noch mal ganz von vorne.

General sports expressions / Allgemeine Ausdrücke im Sport

- Ready, steady, go! (Also: On your marks, get set, go!) — Auf die Plätze, fertig, los!
- She made it into the finals and became the youngest runner-up ever. — zweiter Sieger
- It's time to play fair and be a good sport! — sei kein Spielverderber
- In tennis, cricket and baseball the umpire oversees rules and regulations. — Schiedsrichter
- In football, boxing, basketball, etc, the referee or ref is in charge of fair play. — Schiedsrichter

Cars / Autos

- Imagine, in the middle of nowhere my car had a flat tire. — Platten; (BE) flat tyre
  No garage / service station nearby! — Werkstatt
  It really drove me nuts. — Ich wurde fast wahnsinnig!
- If you ask me, the best service in town is at the gasstation on Forrest Park Avenue, just two minutes from here. — Tankstelle, (BE) petrol station

– I usually fill up the tank and check the oil and brake fluid before driving up north with a borrowed / rented car.	normalerweise; Ölstand prüfen
– I'd like to rent a small size car for two weeks and unlimited mileage.	freie Kilometer

Car enthusiastics / Autofans

– I just love their new sports car. It accelerates in no time.	im Nu
– I think the car makers should come up with an idea. If you ask me, most modern car types look very much the same.	sich etwas einfallen lassen
– My car is a real lemon. I doubt that it will pass inspection.	Ich habe ein richtiges Montagsauto.
– It's a real treat to drive a longer distance in an air-conditioned car.	ein wahrer Genuss; mit Klimaanlage
– Our new car is a stick shift. I'm not too fond of it because now I have trouble backing the car out of the garage.	Wagen mit Gangschaltung, rückwärts aus der Garage fahren.
– The latest model of the S class is a convertible with airbags and air conditioning as standards. The car's a dream.	Cabriolet; Ein Traum von einem Auto!

Traveling by car / Autoreisen

– Our weekend was nothing special. We drove our old station wagon to visit our parents in the countryside.	war nicht besonders; Kombi(wagen);
– The country road was pretty windy and suddenly there was a moose that seemed to appear from nowhere.	kurvig aus dem Nichts auftauchen
– This year's family reunion will be at my cousin's. She lives out in the middle of nowhere with no bus station nearby.	ganz weit draußen
– Thus, we need to rent some mini vans to get the whole gang up there.	somit / folglich
– This isn't out of your way? – No absolutely not; I live just three blocks away.	Das ist kein Umweg für Sie?
– Honey, let's turn around: I'm afraid we missed the right exit.	umdrehen Abzweigung

Generell Car-related Topics / Allgemeines zum Auto

– We really got a very good deal on our second car: I advise you to take your time and shop around. It's worth it.	Ich rate Ihnen sich umsehen.
– Whenever my husband and his best friend talk shop about cars, I take my leave because I don't have the slightest idea what they are talking about.	fachsimpeln nicht die geringste Ahnung haben.

– If you ask me, the trouble in any country of huge dimensions is an underdeveloped public transportation system.
  wenn Sie mich fragen; das Problem ist
– I'm always on the go. I feel like the parental chauffeur, getting my kids from here to there.
  unterwegs sein;

Kulturelle und sprachliche Tipps

Das Wetter

Auch wenn das Wetter immer für einen kleinen Kommentar gut ist, sollte man nicht vergessen, dass das Wetterempfinden kulturell sehr unterschiedlich geprägt ist. Wer in Arizona lebt, ist 40-45 Grad Celsius (104–122 Grad Fahrenheit), dry heat (trockene Hitze) gewöhnt. High humidity (hohe Luftfeuchtigkeit) von 70 und mehr Prozent kann allerdings schon 25 Grad Celsius (77 Grad Fahrenheit) als unangenehm warm erscheinen lassen.

Wenn Sie centigrade nach Fahrenheit umrechnen wollen, nehmen Sie die Celsius-Temperatur mal neun, dividieren das Ergebnis durch fünf und addieren den Faktor 32. Umgekehrt ziehen Sie den Faktor 32 ab, multiplizieren mit fünf und teilen dann durch neun. D.h. 25 Grad Celsius sind in etwa 77 Fahrenheit und 5 Grad Fahrenheit sind in etwa minus 15 Grad Celsius.

Falsche Freunde

Wer an die Straße Unter den Linden oder die Champs-Elysées denkt, sieht eine Prachtstraße mit Bäumen vor seinem inneren Auge. Im Englischen ist eine breite Straße ein boulevard, wenn der von Bäumen gesäumt ist, handelt es sich um eine avenue. Alley heißt die enge Gasse einer Altstadt oder der enge Pfad hinter den Häusern, wo die Mülleimer stehen.

Banale und stumpfsinnige Aufgaben heißen im Englischen mundane tasks. Wer aber von einem *mondänen* Seebad träumt, der sollte besser sagen: fashionable sea-side resort. Um zu Hause schöne Bilder der ausländischen Kollegen vorzeigen zu können, sollte die Kamera ein hochwertiges *Objektiv* (a high-quality lens) haben. Bilder und Eindrücke hingegen sind nie *objektiv*, dann wäre ja alles sehr langweilig. Doch kommt natürlich jeder auf seine Weise ans Ziel: People reach their objectives in their own different ways.

The dome of the church is lovely – damit ist die Kuppel der Kirche gemeint, nicht der Dom. Der Kölner Dom als Hauptkirche einer Diözese ist mit cathedral of Cologne zu übersetzen.

Some berries taste bitter, nämlich herb. Im Garten heißt es aber: Dill ist the only herb I grew this year - Dill ist das einzige Kraut, das ich dieses Jahr angebaut habe. Daneben gibt es aber viele evergreens (immergrüne Pflanzen) im Garten. Wenn eine band allerdings nur evergreens, nämlich alte Lieblingsschlager spielt, dann ist der Gärtner zum Fest eingeladen.

Im englischen und amerikanischen Schulsystem geht jeder auf das Gymnasium (high school), aber nur derjenige, der gerne Sport treibt und fit werden möchte geht ins gymnasium, nämlich die Turnhalle.

List of Useful Expressions /Nützliche Redewendungen

acknowledge	I acknowledge the receipt quittieren; the lawyer acknowledged the document beglaubigen
agree	I agree to come with you ich bin bereit mitzukommen; you will agree that du musst zugeben, dass; let us agree to differ! ich fürchte, wir können uns da nicht einigen!; it is agreed es ist vereinbart, es steht fest; beer does not agree with me; Bier bekommt mir nicht
appreciate	I appreciate the chat with you Ich schätze unser kurzes Gespräch; appreciate music an Musik Gefallen finden; I appreciate your kindness ich bin dankbar für Ihre Freundlichkeit
ask	we were asked to believe man wollte uns glauben machen; ask someone in jemanden hereinbitten; that is asking too much! das ist zuviel verlangt; the matter asks for great care die Sache erfordert große Sorgfalt; you asked for it du wolltest es ja so haben;

believe (in)	I do not believe in sports ich halte nicht viel von Sport; believe it or not ob Sie es glauben oder nicht! would you believe it! nicht zu glauben!; he is believed to be a miser man hält ihn für einen Geizhals;
concern	I am not concerned es geht mich nichts an; to whom it may concern an alle, die es angeht; don't let that concern you mache dir deswegen keine Sorgen!; concern yourself with your problems kümmere dich um deine Probleme; that is no concern of mine das ist nicht meine Sache;
confirm	confirm someone in his role jemanden in seiner Rolle bestärken; confirm one's power seine Macht festigen;
consider	consider his age! bedenke sein Alter!; all things considered wenn man alles in Betracht zieht; he never considers others er nimmt keine Rücksicht auf andere; consider someone a fool: jemanden für einen Narren halten; you may consider yourself lucky du kannst dich glücklich schätzen; consider yourself at home tun Sie, als ob Sie zu Hause wären;
come	be long in coming lange auf sich warten lassen; come to see us besuche uns; come what may! komme, was da wolle!; a year ago come March im März vor einem Jahr; I was coming to that darauf wollte ich

	gerade hinaus; how come? wie kommt das?, wieso (denn)?; nothing came of it es wurde nichts daraus; it comes hard (easy) to me es fällt mir schwer (leicht); how did you come to do that? wie kamen Sie dazu, das zu tun?; in the years to come in den kommenden Jahren;
dare	how dare you say that? wie können Sie es wagen, das zu sagen? I dare say ich glaube wohl; I dare you! du traust dich ja nicht!; I dare you to deny it wage nicht, es abzustreiten.
delight	I am (oder shall be) delighted to come ich komme mit dem größten Vergnügen
do	what can I do for you? womit kann ich dienen?; what does he do for a living? womit verdient er sein Brot?; do business Geschäfte machen; do it into German es ins Deutsche übersetzen; do 60 miles per hour 60 Meilen die Stunde fahren; he did all the talking er führte das große Wort; these pills do me (no) good diese Pillen helfen mir (nicht); will this glass do you? genügt Ihnen dieses Glas?; he was pretty well done er war am Ende seiner Kräfte; nothing doing! es ist nichts los; nichts zu machen!; it's do or die now! jetzt geht's ums Ganze!; do badly schlecht daran sein, schlecht mit etwas fahren; will this quality

do? reicht diese Qualität aus?; it will do tomorrow es hat Zeit bis morgen; that won't do das genügt nicht;

help — help someone to something jemandem bei Tisch etwas reichen; help oneself sich bedienen, zugreifen; I can't help it ich kann nichts dafür; it can't be helped es läßt sich nicht ändern; if I can help it wenn ich es vermeiden kann; she can't help her eyes für ihre Augen kann sie nichts; I could not help laughing ich musste einfach lachen; I can't help feeling ich werde das Gefühl nicht los; I can't help myself ich kann nicht anders; don't stay longer than you can help! bleib nicht länger als nötig!

impress — be favourably impressed by einen guten Eindruck erhalten von; I am not impressed das imponiert mir gar nicht; he is not easily impressed er läßt sich nicht so leicht beeindrucken;

imagine — you can't imagine my joy; du kannst dir meine Freude nicht vorstellen; you can't imagine how ... du machst dir kein Bild, wie ...; you are imagining things! du bildest dir das nur ein!; don't imagine that I am satisfied glaub nicht, ich sei zufrieden; just imagine! stell dir vor!, denk (dir) nur!

know — know what's what genau Bescheid wissen; don't I know it! und ob ich das weiß!; I wouldn't know! das kann ich leider nicht sagen!; for all I know soviel ich weiß; I would have you know that ich möchte Ihnen klarmachen, dass; I have never known him to lie meines Wissens hat er nie gelogen; he knows a thing or two er ist nicht von gestern; he has known better days er hat bessere Tage gesehen; I have known it to happen ich habe das schon erlebt; I should know him anywhere ich würde ihn überall erkennen; before you know where you are im Handumdrehen; let me know laß es mich wissen; you ought to know better das sollten Sie besser wissen; be in the know Bescheid wissen;

lack — he lacks time er hat keine Zeit; he lacked for nothing es fehlte ihm an nichts;

land — land someone in difficulties jemanden in Schwierigkeiten etc. bringen, verwickeln: land someone with something jemandem etwas aufhalsen oder einbrocken; land a good contract einen guten Vertrag an Land ziehen;

mind — mind one's P's and Q's sich ganz gehörig in acht nehmen; mind you learn denk daran zu lernen; mind the step! Achtung, Stufe!; mind the children sich um die Kinder kümmern, die Kinder hüten; mind your own business! kümmere dich um deine eigenen Dinge!; don't mind me! laß dich durch mich nicht stören!; do you mind my smoking? haben Sie etwas dagegen, wenn ich rauche?; would you mind coming? würden Sie so freundlich sein zu kommen?; I don't mind (it) ich habe nichts dagegen, meinetwegen; I wouldn't mind a drink ich hätte nichts gegen einen Drink; never mind! lass es gut sein; he minds a great deal er ist allerdings dagegen;

miss — miss the point das Wesentliche nicht begreifen; he just missed being drowned er wäre beinahe ertrunken; I just missed running him over ich hätte ihn beinahe überfahren; a miss is as good as a mile knapp daneben ist auch vorbei; give something a miss von etwas die Finger lassen;

need — it needs all your strength es erfordert deine ganze Kraft; it needed doing es musste getan werden; it needs but to become known es braucht nur bekannt zu werden;

object (to) — do you object to my leaving? haben Sie etwas dagegen, wenn ich gehe?; if you don't object wenn Sie nichts dagegen haben;

oblige — I was obliged to go ich musste gehen; much obliged! danke bestens!; I am obliged to you for it ich habe es Ihnen zu verdanken; will you oblige me by doing something? wären Sie so freundlich, etwas zu tun?; an early reply will oblige um baldige Antwort wird gebeten;

pardon — pardon me! Verzeihung!; pardon me for interrupting you! entschuldigen Sie, wenn ich Sie unterbreche!; a thousand pardons ich bitte Sie tausendmal um Entschuldigung;

reach — reach something down etwas herunterreichen; reach an understanding eine Einigung erreichen; reach no conclusion zu keinem Schluß gelangen; make a reach for something nach etwas greifen oder langen; within reach erreichbar; above reach unerreichbar, unerschwinglich; within easy reach of the office vom Büro aus leicht zu erreichen;

read — read something into a phrase etwas in einen Satz hineinlesen; do you read me? haben Sie mich verstanden?; we can take it as read that wir können (also) davon ausgehen, dass; I read you like a book ich durchschaue dich; read up on sich einlesen, einarbeiten;

satisfy — satisfy one's curiosity seine Neugier stillen; satisfy the debt die Schuld begleichen, tilgen; I am satisfied that ich bin davon überzeugt, dass;

seem — pears seem not to grow here Pfirsiche wachsen hier anscheinend nicht; it seems as though es sieht so aus als ob; it seems to me that it will rain mir scheint, es wird regnen; it should seem that man sollte glauben, dass; I can't seem to open the package ich bringe dieses Packet einfach nicht auf;

suppose — it is to be supposed that es ist anzunehmen, dass; suppose we went for a walk! wie wäre es, wenn wir einen Spaziergang machten!: suppose you meet me at 10 o'clock ich schlage vor, du triffst mich um 10 Uhr; I don't suppose we shall be back ich glaube nicht, dass wir zurück sein werden; isn't he supposed to be at the meeting? sollte er nicht eigentlich bei der Besprechung sein?; what is that supposed to be? was soll das sein?

think — think ahead vorausdenken, vorsichtig sein; now that I come to think of it dabei fällt mir ein; think highly of viel halten von; think nothing of wenig halten von; I should think so das will ich meinen; think something over sich etwas durch den Kopf gehen lassen; think up sich etwas einfallen lassen; think oneself clever sich für klug halten; I think it best ich halte es für das Beste; think no harm nichts Böses denken; have a think about something etwas überdenken

trouble — May I trouble you to pass me the salt? Darf ich Sie um das Salz bitten; don't let it trouble you machen Sie sich deswegen keine Gedanken; troubled face sorgenvolles Gesicht; troubled waters schwierige Situation, unangenehme Lage;

don't trouble to write du brauchst nicht zu schreiben;

welcome — make someone welcome jemanden herzlich empfangen; you are welcome to it Es steht zu Ihrer Verfügung; you are welcome to do it das können Sie gerne tun;

will / would — will you pass me the bread, please? reichen Sie mir doch bitte das Brot!; boys will be boys Jungen sind nun einmal so; as you will! wie du willst; he would not go er wollte einfach nicht gehen; he would take a walk every day er pflegte täglich einen Spaziergang zu machen; you would do that! das sieht dir ähnlich; it would seem that es scheint fast, dass;

wish	wish oneself home sich nach Hause sehnen; it is to be wished es steht zu hoffen; wish someone well jemandem wohlwollen; wish someone ill jemandem übelwollen; she cannot wish for anything better sie kann sich nichts Besseres wünschen;
wonder	it is not to be wondered at es ist nicht verwunderlich; I wonder whether I might ...? dürfte ich vielleicht...?; I wonder if you could help me vielleicht können Sie mir helfen;

Stichwortverzeichnis

Ausstellung 67ff., 76f.
Autos 106ff., 109f.
- Allgemeines 111f.
- Autofans 110
- Autoreisen 75, 111

Bedanken 31f.
Begrüßung 8ff., 27, 44f., 48
Büro/Arbeitsplatz 36ff., 48f., 54, 56f.

Charakter 41 f.

Einkaufen 69ff., 77
- Bücher 71
- Drogerie 71f.
- Kleider 70
- Lebensmittel 70f.
Einladung 16ff., 28ff.
Empfang 15
Essen 15, 20, 29
- Beschwerden 25
- Bitten 25f.
- Essen gehen 23ff., 32f.
- Essensgewohnheiten 29

Dank 31f.

Fahrenheit 112
Familie 97ff.
Ferien 85f.
Fernsehen 30
Film 64ff.
- Filmkritik 65f.
Freizeit 94f.

Garten 97ff., 101ff.
Gastgeschenke 29
Geburtstage 49 ff.,
Gruppe 11

Haus 20f., 45
Haustiere 97ff., 104f.
Hobby 92ff.
Höflichkeit 38f., 55f.

Interessen 95f.

Jubiläum 52

Kaffeepause 47 f.
Kinder 97 ff.
Kino 64ff, 76
Kollegen 48f.
Komplimente 20, 39, 42, 54f.
Konversation
- Abschluss 13
- Anfang 12
Konzert 60ff., 76
Kultur 59 ff.
Kunden 43ff.

Länder 30f., 84ff.
- besondere Namen 88
- Länderbeschreibung 90
- Landschaftsbeschreibung 87f.
- Touristeninformation 90f.
- Wegbeschreibung 91
Literatur 64ff.

Museum 67ff., 76f.
Musik 94f.

Party 49ff.
- Geburtstag 52f.
- Jubiläum 52
- Weihnachten 53f., 56f.
Personenbeschreibung 39ff.
- Haar 40f.
- Körper 40f.
Pünktlichkeit 30 f.

Reisen 73ff., 84ff.
- Autoreisen 75, 111
- Busreisen 74f.
- Flugreisen 74
- Reisekommentare 86f.
- Schiffsreisen 75
Restaurant 24 ff., 32
Räumlichkeiten 45

Sekretärinnentag 53
Spiele 93f.
Sport 106ff.
- allgemeine Ausdrücke 109
- Ausrüstung 108
- Redewendungen 108f.
- Sportarten 107f.
Städte 84ff.
-Städtebeschreibung 89

Tagung 13ff.
Theater 62ff., 76
Treffen, formloses 27, 48, 54

Verabschiedung 21ff., 51f.
Vortrag 47f.

Weihnachten 53, 56
Wetter 80ff., 112

Clevere Business Tools für anspruchsvolle Lösungen

Moderation

Das Haufe Business Tool ist Ihre ideale Arbeitshilfe, mit der Sie Mitarbeiter, Teams oder Projektgruppen in Besprechungen zum Erfolg führen – auch wenn's im Team mal kritisch werden sollte.

- Praxiserprobte Methoden und Werkzeuge für jede Moderationsphase sofort zur Hand
- Prozesspläne, Agenden und Tipps unterstützen beim Ablauf
- Praxisbeispiele mit Lösungsvorschlägen helfen, auf Konflikte schnell zu reagieren
- Nützliche Arbeitshilfen, wie z.B. Checklisten, Übersichten und Formulare für alle Moderationsphasen
- Moderationsplaner im DIN A1-Format

Die CD-ROM bietet alle Moderations-Tools, Formulare, Übersichten und Checklisten als Vorlage zum Ausdrucken oder zum Kopieren auf Folie. Damit sind Sie bestens für jede Moderation vorbereitet und führen Ihr Team souverän.

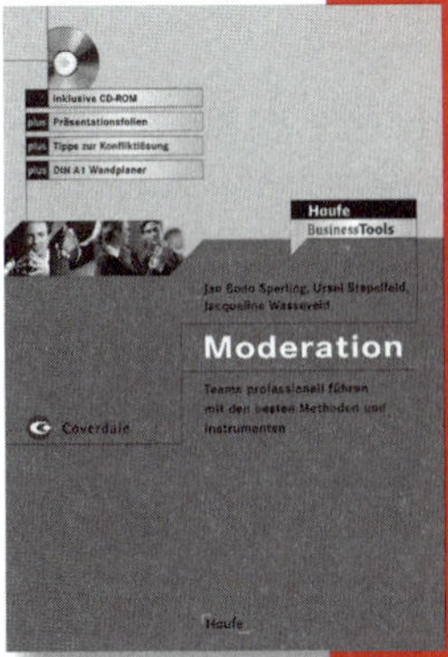

Moderation
Teams professionell führen mit den besten Methoden und Instrumenten
inkl. CD-ROM
€ 78,–*
Bestell-Nr. 00800-0001
ISBN 3-448-05642-1

* *inkl. MwSt., zzgl. Versandpauschale € 1,90*

Bestellen Sie bei Ihrer Buchhandlung oder direkt beim Verlag:
Haufe Service Center GmbH, Postfach, 79091 Freiburg
Tel.: 0180/5050440*, Fax: 0180/5050441* * 12 Cent pro Minute
Internet: www.haufe.de
E-Mail: bestellung@haufe.de